Wilderness Survival

Wilderness Survival

Gregory J. Davenport

STACKPOLE
BOOKS

Published by
STACKPOLE BOOKS
5067 Ritter Road
Mechanicsburg, PA 17055

Printed in the United States

10 9 8 7 6 5 4 3 2 1

First edition

Although *Wilderness Survival* provides extremely valuable information, it cannot guarantee survival. Misuse of some of the information in this book may lead to both physical and equipment damage, for which the author disclaims any liability.

Library of Congress Cataloging-in Publication Data

Davenport, Gregory J.
    Wilderness Survival / Gregory J. Davenport. — 1st ed
      p.   cm.
    ISBN 0-8117-2985-0 (pbk.)
    1. Wilderness survival Handbooks, manuals, etc. I. Title.
GV200.5.D38   1997
613.6'9—DC21   97-24515
                                                CIP

This book is dedicated to all the men and women of the USAF Survival School, past and present, who teach others the valuable skills of survival, especially to my good friends and fellow instructors MSgt Robert Milks (Uncle Bob) and SMSgt Rick Arnold (Face).

Thanks to Neil Felgenhauer, Ed Powell, Dr. Robert Wooten, Steve Davenport, and Jackie Davenport for their help throughout this whole process. Special thanks to Steve for his work on all the illustrations contained within. Last but not least, I'd like to thank my family—Kim, Jamie, and Jenna. Without their support and strength, I'd never have finished this project. Kim was extremely valuable as an editor and friend. She was instrumental in helping this book mature from an idea to what it is today.

Contents

Introduction		**1**
1.	**CLIMATES OF THE GLOBE**	**5**
	Tropical	5
	Dry	6
	Warm Temperate	6
	Snow	8
	Ice	8
2.	**PERSONAL PROTECTION**	**10**
	Clothing	10
	Clothing maintenance	10
	Sleeping bag	12
	Improvised clothing and equipment	12
	Shelter	18
	Site selection	18
	Types of emergency shelters and their construction	18
	Bedding	31
	Fire	31
	Purposes of fire	31
	Building a fire	31
	Banking the fire	47
	Cutting tools	48

3. SIGNALING   **50**
   Signal Location   50
   Types of Signals and How to Use Them   50
     Manufactured signaling devices   50
     Improvised signaling devices   56

4. SUSTENANCE   **62**
   Water   62
     Water requirements   62
     Water sources and how to procure water   63
     Water preparation   72
     Water storage   75
     Water conservation   75
     Liquids to avoid   75
   Food   76
     Need for food   76
     Food sources: procurement and preparation   76
     Methods of cooking food   107
     Food preservation   108
     Food storage   111
     Emergency food   111

5. TRAVEL AND NAVIGATION   **112**
   Tools of Navigation   112
     Map nomenclature   112
     Compass nomenclature   119
   Using a Map and Compass Together   121
     Determine general location   121
     Orienting the map with a compass   121
     Triangulating to pinpoint your location   124
   Determining and Maintaining a Field Bearing   126
     Establishing a field bearing   126
     Staying on route during travel   128
   Determining Direction Without a Compass   129
     Using constellations to determine direction   129

Using a stick and shadow to determine direction	130
Using a watch to determine direction	133
Additional Information on Travel	135
Energy conservation	135
Terrain considerations	135
Leaving word	136
Packing your gear for ease of travel	136
6. HEALTH	**137**
General Health Issues	137
Staying hydrated	137
Nourishment	138
Cleanliness	138
Rest	139
Traumatic Injuries and Their Treatment	140
Airway, breathing, circulation (ABCs)	140
Bleeding (hemorrhage)	143
Shock	144
Injuries to the head	145
Fractures	146
Injuries of joints and muscles	147
Burns	148
Foreign bodies in the eye	149
Wounds, lacerations, and infections	150
Environmental Injuries and Illnesses	150
Cold injuries	150
Immersion injuries (trench foot)	153
Snow blindness	153
Heat injuries	154
Altitude illness	155
Snake and animal bites	159
Intestinal parasites	160
Insect bites and stings	160
Other Wilderness Problems	161
Blisters	161

Thorns and splinters   161
Diarrhea   162
Constipation   162
Cold or flu   162
Heat rash   162
Survival Stress   163
Components of survival stress   163
Overcoming survival stress   165

Appendix A: Knots and Lashes   **168**
Appendix B: Survival and Medical Emergency Gear   **171**
References and Recommended Reading   **173**
Index   **174**

Introduction

The elk he'd been tracking was nowhere in sight; he wondered why he'd kept following it for so long. Less than forty-eight hours ago, he'd been comfortably sleeping in a warm king-size bed. Now he lay in a fetal position under a sparsely covered pine tree. The tree provided little protection from the cold, damp snow that flurried around him. His clothes were soaked. He was shivering and couldn't seem to stop.

Earlier attempts at starting a fire had failed when his wet matches wouldn't light. "Why didn't I carry more emergency survival gear?" he asked himself. Before leaving the comforts of home, he'd filled his car with all the modern camping necessities: a large Coleman stove, an ornate kerosene lamp, a colorful expensive tent, and a top-of-the-line down sleeping bag. He hadn't bothered to pack an emergency survival or first-aid kit. He had never needed one before.

For Mark, the day had started like so many others. At 5 A.M. his friend Jake could be heard rustling around the camp, breaking wood and starting a fire. He counted on Jake to build a hair-singeing fire every morning. Jake loved fires so much that Mark often wondered if he was a closet pyromaniac. He didn't use matches, opting to use a metal match instead. Mark thought it seemed silly to use such a primitive device when both matches and lighters were available. But Jake, sticking true to his convictions, often said, "Matches and lighters run out, but a metal match will last forever." Secretly, Mark often wished he had Jake's talent for building fires.

Mark hated getting out of his sleeping bag in the morning, especially on a cold day like this. He waited until the fire crackled and then jumped from his bag and ran toward it as fast as his bare feet could safely take him. Sitting on a wet, cold log, Mark attempted to put on his socks and boots. The

1

leather boots had been left out all night. They were slightly frozen and stiff, and he was unable to get them over his thick wool socks. Although he knew better, Mark decided to wear a thin pair of cotton socks that he'd brought along for the ride home. He was sure they wouldn't get wet.

Breakfast was quick—a peanut butter and jelly sandwich washed down with a coffee mug full of beer and tomato juice, a long-standing tradition. After eating, Mark began packing his gear. Staying close to the fire in order to keep warm, he organized a small fanny pack full of all the things he felt were necessary for a day of hunting: a bag of red licorice, four granola bars, matches, ammunition, a knife, and a quart of water. Mark always traveled light, believing it was necessary to conserve his strength to pack out the elk he intended to kill. He would laugh at Jake, who carried a small summit pack full of gear; it seemed unreasonable to carry so much.

Mark said good-bye to Jake as he left camp, feeling high on the morning air and sure today would be his day to return with an elk in tow. When Jake asked for his itinerary, Mark said he was going to play it by ear and really didn't have any special plans for the day. He felt so comfortable with his knowledge of the surrounding terrain that he didn't even carry a map or compass. He often bragged about this to his friends and made fun of them for carrying a compass and map into the same old forest where they'd hunted for so many years.

Within minutes of departing camp, Mark spotted a majestic seven-point elk feeding on the dew-fresh grass of a nearby meadow. Caught unprepared, he was unable to chamber a round before the elk spooked and cascaded into the surrounding forest. Sure of his tracking skills, he excitedly headed into the woods after the evasive creature. Several hours of searching passed before Mark stopped and suddenly realized he'd lost track of his location. Unwilling to abandon the hunt, he decided to continue until 3 P.M. If he was unable to locate the elk by then, he thought, he'd get to high ground and look for a familiar landmark by which to find his way back to camp.

At around 2 P.M., the weather began to change drastically. The temperature quickly dropped below freezing, and a thick fog descended. Mark felt as if he'd been placed inside a large cooler that was without lighting or windows; the cold air was bone-chilling, and he couldn't see more than 5 feet ahead of him. The elk he'd been tracking was long gone. He was still unaware of his present location, and as there were no visible landmarks, the way back to camp was uncertain. Shortly after the fog settled, Mother Nature decided it was time to show her teeth and delivered an unyielding downpour of rain and snow. Mark wished he had brought his rain gear. As the temperature continued to drop, Mark started to sense his predicament and began to frantically wander around in circles looking for a landmark or any sign of his hunting party. Panic began to set in, and the rhythmic beat of his pounding heart was so loud he thought his head would explode.

Darkness fell. In an attempt to alert his comrades of his desperate situation, Mark fired three rounds from his rifle every five minutes until his ammunition was gone. Cold, wet, and freezing, he crawled under a large lodgepole pine and tried to keep warm, but to no avail. His attempts to build a fire failed because his matches had become wet. He had no matches, no fire, no change of clothing, no navigational tools, and no improvising skills with which to meet his needs.

Crying and scared, he recalled how he'd read of a hiker who had died two years earlier from the effects of hypothermia while camping under conditions similar to these. When reading the article, he'd wondered how it could have happened and questioned the experience of the hiker. He now understood his own vulnerabilities and wished he'd been better prepared. As the hours passed, hypothermia's overwhelming cloud began to take hold, and Mark started drifting off to sleep. His thoughts became peaceful, wondering if his family would miss him; if his body would be found before Christmas; and if another hunter might read of his death and question, as he'd done of the hiker, his experience as a wilderness traveler.

Although extreme, this scenario is not unheard of. Every year wilderness travelers make one or more mistakes similar to those made by Mark, and for some it may even lead to death. Learning to survive in the wilderness is a skill not only for hunters but also for those who raft, fish, hike, climb, ski, four-wheel drive, forage, and so on. You can't predict where or when you might find yourself in a survival situation, and that's why preparation is of paramount importance for all backcountry travelers. If people like Mark had known the five essentials of wilderness survival, they might have lived. *Wilderness Survival* covers these principles and has been written to aid all backcountry travelers regardless of the climate and environment they might be in.

Since humankind's departure from nature, most individuals have lost their innate ability to survive in the wilderness. (When was the last time you killed an animal and used it for food, clothing, and tools?) In modern civilization, the basic requirements of living are taken for granted. In a survival situation, these needs must not only be recognized but also be met. The five basic elements of wilderness survival are personal protection (clothing, shelter, and fire), signaling, sustenance (water and food), travel, and health (dealing with traumatic injuries, environmental injuries, and stress). This book will explore the process of wilderness living and explain the various methods of meeting each survival need.

1

Climates of the Globe

Since proper prior preparation prevents poor performance (the six Ps of survival), all wilderness enthusiasts should learn about the pros and cons of each environment prior to traveling in it. This chapter outlines the five major climates and lists the basic characteristics of each.

CLIMATES OF THE GLOBE

TROPICAL

Location
Most tropical rain forests are between 23.5 degrees north latitude and 23.5 degrees south latitude.

Distinguishing Characteristics
Tropical climates can be found in rain forests, mangrove or other swamps, open grassy plains, or semidry brushlands. In the tropical rain forest, the vegetation can be from three to five stories with an upper canopy of trees ranging from 150 to 180 feet high. The density of the underlying layers depends upon how much sun penetrates the upper canopy. The more sun that gets through, the greater the density.

Average Temperature Each Month
Greater than 64.5° F.

Average Precipitation
Greater than 80 inches per year, and exceeds annual evaporation.

Examples
Jungles of South America, Asia, and Africa.

Problems for the Survivor
Insects, steep terrain, extreme moisture, and difficulty finding an appropriate signaling site.

DRY

Location
Most dry climates (deserts) are between 15 degrees and 35 degrees latitude on each side of the equator.

Distinguishing Characteristics
Deserts are usually alkali, rock, or sand. Some are completely barren, whereas others have grass and thorny bushes throughout.

Average Temperature Each Month
Deserts have wide temperature swings, and it's not uncommon to see extremely hot days and cold nights.

Average Precipitation
Usually less than 10 inches per year.

Examples
Sahara, Gobi, and Mojave Deserts.

Problems for the Survivor
Difficulty in finding water, and the extreme temperature changes between day and night.

WARM TEMPERATE

Location
Most temperate zones are between 23.5 degrees and 66.5 degrees latitude on each side of the equator.

The dry desert climate can pose many challenges to a survivor.

Distinguishing Characteristics
There are two main temperate environments: the temperate oceanic climate, which gets high precipitation; and the continental climate, which has more of a seasonal temperature variance.

Average Temperature Each Month
Both winter and summer seasons are usually without extremes.

Average Precipitation
Varies from 10 to 300 inches, depending on which temperate climate you're in. The highest precipitation is seen in the temperate oceanic climates.

Examples
Olympic and Rocky Mountains and the Cascade Range.

Problems for the Survivor
Probably the best environment in which a survivor can meet his needs.

SNOW

Location
Between 35 degrees and 70 degrees north latitude.

Distinguishing Characteristics
There are two snow climates: the continental subarctic, where freezing temperatures occur six to seven months of the year and the ground is frozen to a depth of several feet; and the humid continental climate, which has only 10 to 40 inches of precipitation (primarily snow) and far fewer temperature extremes than the continental subarctic. Both have seasonal extremes of daylight and darkness.

Average Temperature Each Month
During the coldest months, less than 26.6°F; during the warmest months, greater than 50°F.

Average Precipitation
May range from 10 to 40 inches.

Examples
Alaska, New England, and the Great Lakes region.

Problems for the Survivor
Extreme cold, difficulty traveling on snow and ice, and problems with battery-operated equipment due to the low temperature.

ICE

Location
Most ice climates are located north of 50 degrees north latitude and south of 45 degrees south latitude.

Distinguishing Characteristics
Ice climates can be broken into three separate, distinct categories: marine subarctic, noted for its high precipitation and strong winds; tundra, which has a layer of permafrost (permanent ground frost) over most of its underbrush; and the ice cap, which is composed of Greenland, Antarctic, and sea ice on the Arctic Ocean (all are either covered with or composed of ice).

Average Temperature Each Month
Warmest months are less than 50°F.

Average Precipitation
Extremely variable.

Examples
Alaska tundra, Greenland.

Problems for the Survivor
Extreme cold, difficulty traveling on ice, problems with battery-operated equipment due to the low temperature, and scarcity of fuel for starting a fire.

2

Personal Protection

Personal protection consists of three distinct categories: clothing, shelter, and fire. Each plays a vital role in protecting us from the harsh realities that can be dealt by nature.

CLOTHING

Clothing is your first line of defense against the environment. In the cold, it insulates you, keeping you warm; in a hot environment, proper clothing helps keep you cool.

CLOTHING MAINTENANCE

The acronym COLDER will help you remember how to wear and maintain your clothes.

C: Clean

Clothes are made of intertwined fibers that, when clean, trap dead air. The trapped air keeps you warm by providing valuable insulation. If clothes are dirty, they lose their insulating ability.

O: Avoid Overheating

Clothes absorb sweat. Once this occurs, they lose their insulating quality. In addition, valuable body heat is lost through evaporation when you become overheated.

L: Loose and Layered

Clothing that is too tight will constrict circulation and predispose you to frostbite. Wearing multiple layers increases the amount of dead air space surrounding the body. It also allows you to add or remove individual layers of clothing as necessary for the given weather conditions. In a cold environment, clothes should be worn in three layers. Suggested options are as follows:

Inner layer—allows for ventilation
• Polypropylene—draws moisture away from the body, dries quickly, and retains most of its insulative qualities when wet.
• Cotton—draws moisture away from the body but has almost no insulation value when wet (not recommended).

Middle layer—insulates by trapping dead air
• Wool—absorbs moisture. Retains most of its insulative value when wet.
• Polyester pile or compressed polyester fleece—similar to wool in structure but pound for pound is thicker and warmer.
• Spun synthetic filament (Dacron, Hollofil II, Polyguard, Thinsulate)—lighter than wool of equivalent dead air thickness. Retains insulative qualities when wet.
• Down—the warmest insulation available, but when wet it collapses and loses its insulative value.

Outermost layer—protects from the wind and rain
• Gore-Tex—provides some ventilation as well as protection from the wind and rain.
• Nylon shell—provides protection from the wind and repels rain and snow. If the nylon is uncoated, the moisture will penetrate the material; if the nylon is coated, chances are you will perspire and ultimately become just as wet.
• Head gear and gloves—these are a must, as one-third to one-half of all body heat loss occurs from the head and hands.

D: Dry
Wet clothes lose their insulative quality. To keep the inner layer dry, avoid sweating. Protect your outer layer from moisture either by avoiding exposure to rain or snow or by wearing proper clothing as listed above. If your clothes do become wet, dry them by a fire or, if available, in the sun. If it's below 32°F and you can't build a fire, let the clothes freeze; once frozen,

break the ice out of the clothing. If snow is on your clothes, shake it off (don't brush it off, as this will force the moisture into the fibers).

E: Examine
Examine all clothing daily for tears, dirt, and so on.

R: Repair
Repair any rips and tears as soon as they occur. This may require a needle and thread, so be sure to pack them.

SLEEPING BAG

General Rules of Use
- Fluff prior to using to create adequate dead air space.
- Fluff every morning and, if the weather permits, air-dry each day.
- Take care to keep down-filled bags dry.

IMPROVISED CLOTHING AND EQUIPMENT

Double Socks

Purpose
To keep the feet dry and warm.

Construction technique—layered principle
- Inner layer: sock.
- Middle layer: feathers, dry grass, man-made cushion padding, or fur held in place by a second sock.
- Outer layer: any nylon or rubber material that can be wrapped around the feet and tied at the ankles.

Gaiters

Purpose
Protect legs from insects and from getting scratched by low underbrush. They also keep shoes free from moisture and dirt.

Greg Davenport demonstrates the COLDER acronym during a trip to northern Montana.

<u>Construction technique</u>
Wrap canvas, poncho material, and/or nylon around the lower leg from the top of the calf to below the ankle.

Snowshoes

<u>Purpose</u>
Distribute your body weight over a greater surface area, which in turn makes traveling on snow easier.

Construction techniques

Trail snowshoe

1. Gather two saplings 5 feet long (1 inch in diameter), lay them side by side, and lash them together at each end.
2. 18 inches back from the front of the snowshoe, spread the saplings and lash a 12-inch stick perpendicular to them. Lash another stick, of similar size, 8 inches beyond the first. (For best results, notch the ends of each stick before lashing.)
3. Lash two more sticks between and perpendicular to the 12-inch ones. Place them approximately 2 inches from each sapling, and don't forget to notch the ends. (The middle space provides an opening for the toe of your boot.)
4. Lash two 10-inch-long sticks to the snowshoe where the heel of your boot rests when its toe is centered in the forward opening. (Once again, notch the sticks for better results.)

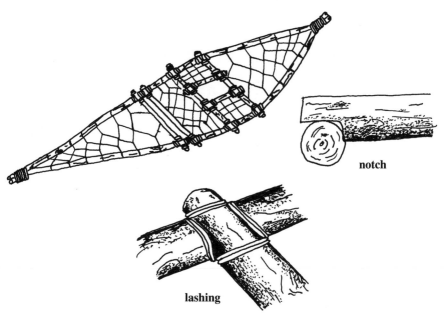

notch

lashing

Improvised trail snowshoe

5. Incorporate parachute line, nylon line, or other durable material in all other space between the two saplings. This will increase the amount of surface area contacting the snow.
6. Bindings: using one piece of line, attach the boot to the snowshoe so that it can pivot while walking. This is done by securing a line to the second stick (from the front) and then wrapping it over the top of the boot and around the heel. Finish by tying the two free ends together.

Bough snowshoe

1. Use boughs from a tree where the smaller branches and needles are thick and abundant (example: fir). Cut five to ten boughs, each 4 to 5 feet long.
2. Lash the base of all the branches together and loosely tie them around their midpoint.
3. Bindings: simply secure the toe of the boot to the forward third of the boughs by tying a line around both.

Sun and/or Snow Goggles

Purpose
To prevent sun- and/or snowblindness.

Construction technique
• Using any shielding material, such as bark, webbing, and/or leather, cut a piece that is as long and wide as necessary to cover both eyes.
• Make small, horizontal slits at the point where the material is directly over each eye.
• Attach line to both sides of the goggles so that when they're tied together they hold the goggles in place.

Tanning an Animal's Hide

Once an animal has been skinned, its hide can be used for many different survivor needs. (Refer to chapter 4 for instructions on how to skin an animal.) If prepared properly, the hide can provide a valuable resource for improvising many different clothing items. (Although it is unlikely you'll find yourself in a survival situation where this information is necessary, it is nevertheless being provided for your reference.) Although there are

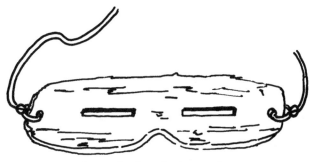

Improvised sun/snow goggles

many ways to tan a hide, some may not be practical for a survivor. One method of preparing a hide for use is as follows:

1. Soak the hide by completely submersing it in untreated water.
    *   One to two hours if you don't intend to remove the hair.
    *   Two to three days if you plan to remove the hair.
    *   Change the water every day.
2. Stretch the hide.
    *   Stretch and stake the hide on a hard, clean, and level surface.
    *   Alternatively, secure it to four branches that have been lashed together to form a rack approximately 6 feet square. The hide is stretched inside the square by creating small holes, 2 to 3 inches apart, in its outer edges and then running line through each hole and around the branches in a continuous fashion. For best results, secure the hide's four edges to the branches first.
    *   Another popular method is to lay the hide on a slanted log that forms a 25- to 30-degree angle between the log, your stomach, and the ground. Since you shouldn't have to bend over to flesh or de-hair hides, the exact log angle will depend on your arm motion as you push down and away when scraping the hide.
    *   If stretching the hide, be sure to retighten it periodically.
3. Scrape the hide.
    *   Remove any excess fat or meat from the hide.
    *   Let the hide dry completely.
    *   Using a dull blade or stone, scrape off the hide's hair and outer membrane, meat side first, by repeatedly applying gentle downward

pressure at 90 degrees to the hide, until it becomes soft and pliable. *Note:* When scraping the hair side, start at the neck and scrape in the direction of hair growth.

4. Tanning the hide.

    Tanning the hide will make it softer and more practical for use as clothing.

    • Soak the hide in water until soft.

    • Using a small fire, warm the animal's brains while continually working them until you're able to smash them into a thick solution.

    • Thoroughly rub the brain solution into the animal's wet hide until it becomes noticeably soft and pliable. If the hair was removed, do both sides.

    • Wring the moisture out of the hide, stretch it tight, and work it with your hand until it's dry. Work both sides if the hair was removed.

5. Finally, use the hide as you would any material to create the clothing necessary for your survival.

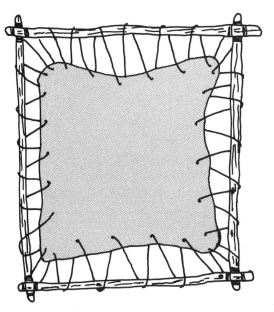

The use of four branches lashed together is one method of stretching an animal hide during the tanning process.

SHELTER

A shelter is your second line of personal protection. Its primary purpose is to protect you from the elements: cold, heat, wet, and wind. The relative importance of a shelter is determined by the climate.

SITE SELECTION

The following are optimal guidelines for selecting a shelter site.

- Close to signal and recovery site (covered in chapter 3).
- Close to food and water sources (covered in chapter 4).
- Large enough and level enough to lie down comfortably.
- Enough materials available to build the shelter you need.

The ideal site will have a southern exposure if it's north of the equator and a northern exposure if south of it; this allows for optimal light and heat from the sun throughout the day. Build your shelter so that the entrance faces east; this allows for the best early-morning sun exposure.

Avoid Environmental Hazards

- Avoid avalanche slopes.
- Avoid drainage and dry riverbeds with a potential for flash floods.
- If near bodies of water, stay above tide marks.
- Avoid rock formations that might collapse.
- Avoid dead trees that might blow down and overhanging dead limbs.
- Avoid animals and their trails.

TYPES OF EMERGENCY SHELTERS
AND THEIR CONSTRUCTION

The type of shelter you construct will be determined by the environment, materials on hand, and the amount of time available. Three shelter types are outlined here: natural, tarp, and tent.

Natural Shelters

A natural shelter is composed of materials that are procured from the wilderness. As with any shelter, its sole purpose is to protect you and your equipment from the elements. Construction techniques for several natural shelters are outlined below. *Note:* The use of natural shelter materials is recommended *only* in an actual survival situation.

Tree pit

A tree pit shelter is most often used in the warm temperate and snow environments.

1. Find a tree with multiple lower branches that provide adequate overhead cover, such as a Douglas or grand fir. Pine trees provide little protection and are not a good choice.
2. Break away the lower branches until there is enough room for both you and your equipment.
3. Incorporate the broken branches into the structure of the tree to provide additional protection from the elements.
4. In the winter, the surrounding snow forms an excellent source of insulation for your tree pit shelter. If possible, dig down to bare ground until you have an area big enough for you and your equipment.

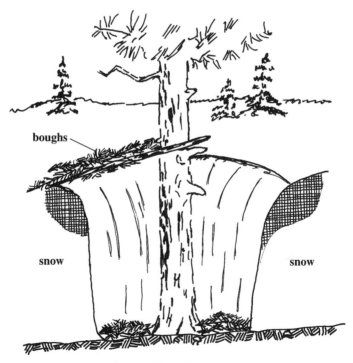

Tree pit

Natural lean-to

Lean-to
A lean-to is most often used in the warm temperate and snow environments.
1. Find two trees about 7 feet apart with forked branches 4 to 5 feet high on the trunk.
2. Break away any other branches that pose a safety threat or interfere with the construction of your lean-to.
3. Place a ridge pole (a fallen tree that is approximately 10 feet long and the diameter of your wrist) into the forked branches. *Note:* If unable to find two trees with forked branches, lash the ridge pole to the trees.
4. Lay several support poles across the ridge pole, at a 45- to 60-degree angle to the ground. Support poles need to be about 10 feet long and placed 1 to 2 feet apart.
5. Crisscross small branches into the support poles.
6. Cover the framework with 8 to 12 inches of grass, moss, boughs, and so forth. The material should be placed in a layered fashion, starting at the bottom.

7. In bad weather, completely enclose the shelter by building another lean-to on the opposite side.

A-Frame
An A-Frame is most often used in the warm temperate and snow environments.
1. Find a tree with a forked branch 3 to 4 feet above the base of the trunk.
2. Break away any other branches that pose a safety threat or interfere with the construction of your A-frame.
3. Place a ridge pole (a fallen tree 12 to 15 feet long and the diameter of your wrist) into the forked branch, forming a 30-degree angle between the pole and the ground. *Note:* If unable to find a tree with a forked branch, lash the ridge pole to the tree. Another option is to locate a fallen tree that's at an approximately 30-degree angle to the ground, or to lay a strong ridge pole against a 3- to 4-foot-high stump.
4. Lay support poles across the ridge pole, on both sides, at a 60-degree angle to the ground. Support poles need to be long enough to extend above the ridge pole and should be placed about 1 to 1½ feet apart.
5. Crisscross small branches into the support poles.
6. Cover the framework with grass, moss, boughs, and so forth. The material should be placed in a layered fashion, starting at the bottom.

Natural A-frame

Platform bed

Platform bed

The platform bed is most often used in the tropical, snow, and warm temperate environments when the ground is wet or small animals or insects are a nuisance.

1. Find three trees that form a triangle, or cut three poles and pound them firmly into the ground so that they form a triangle. The long sides of the triangle must be at least 7 feet long.
2. Cut two poles 1 foot longer than the triangle's sides, and lash them to the trees or poles several feet above the ground. Make sure they are strong enough to support your weight.
3. Create a solid platform by laying additional poles on top of and perpendicular to the side poles. Make sure they are strong enough to support your weight.
4. For added comfort and insulation, cover the top of the platform with 12 to 18 inches of dry moss, leaves, grass, and so forth.
5. If you have a tarp or poncho, construct an elevated A-tent above the bed (covered under tarp shelters below).

Hobo shelter

A hobo shelter is most often used in the temperate oceanic environments, where a more stable long-term shelter is necessary. Its construction is dependent on procuring multiple pieces of driftwood and boards that have washed ashore.

1. Using a sand dune that's out of high tide's reach, dig a rectangular space on the land side of the dune (not on the side that faces the beach) that is big enough for both you and your equipment. Place the removed sand close by so that you can use it later.
2. Using several pieces of driftwood, parachute line, nylon line, or other durable material, build a strong frame inside the rectangular dugout.
3. Attach driftwood and boards around and above the entire frame, leaving a doorway through which to enter and exit the shelter. If the amount of wood available is limited, don't frame in the sides or back of the structure (although some sand may fall into the shelter if it doesn't have four walls around it).
4. If you have a poncho or tarp that's not necessary for meeting your other needs, consider placing it over the roof.
5. Now cover the roof with 6 to 8 inches of the sand you removed from the dugout to help insulate the shelter.

Hobo shelter

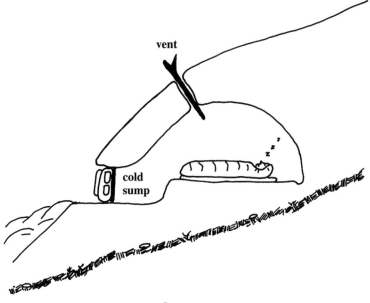

Snow cave

Snow cave
A snow cave is most often used in the warm temperate (winter) and snow
environments.

1. Find an area with firm snow at a depth of at least 6 feet (a steep slope
   such as a riverbank or a snowdrift will suffice, provided it is not at risk
   of an avalanche).
2. Dig an entryway into the slope deep enough to start a tunnel (approximately 3 feet) and wide enough for you to fit into.
3. Since cold air sinks, construct a snow platform 2 to 3 feet above the
   entryway. It should be flat, level, and large enough for you to comfortably
   lie down on.
4. Using the entryway as a starting point, hollow out a domed area that is
   large enough for you and your equipment. To prevent the ceiling from
   settling or falling in on you, create a high domed roof.
5. To prevent asphyxiation, make a ventilation hole in the roof. If available,
   insert a stick or pole through the hole so that it can be cleared periodically.

6. To further protect the shelter from the elements, place your pack in the entryway.
7. Since you are oblivious to the conditions outside, check the entrance periodically.

Note: The temperature must be well below freezing to ensure that the walls of the cave will stay firm and the snow will not melt. In addition, once the snow shelter is built, never get the temperature above freezing inside; if this happens, it will lose its insulation quality and you will get wet from the subsequent moisture. A general rule is that if you can't see your breath, it's too warm. Remember the COLDER principles and avoid overheating during the construction process.

Snow A-frame
A snow A-frame is an alternative to the snow cave that is most often used in the warm temperate winter, snow, and ice environments.
1. Find an 8-by-4-foot flat area that is clear of trees and underbrush. (The snow must be at least 3 to 4 feet deep.)
2. Stomp out a rectangular platform wide and long enough to accommodate your body.
3. Let it harden for at least thirty minutes.
4. Dig a 3-foot-deep entryway just in front of the rectangular area.
5. Evacuate the compacted snow by cutting multiple 3-foot-square blocks that are 8 to 10 inches wide (this will require an instrument such as a large machete, stick, or ski).

Snow A-frame

6. Once the blocks have been removed, place them one against another to form an A-frame above the trench.
7. Fill in any gaps with surrounding snow.

Tarp Shelters
A tarp is made of a light, inexpensive material that provides adequate shelter in most wilderness settings. Construction techniques for several tarp shelters are outlined below.

A-tent design
An A-tent is most often used in the warm temperate and snow environments.
1. Tightly secure a ridge line 3 to 4 feet above the ground and between two objects that are approximately 7 feet apart.
2. Drape the tarp over the stretched line.
3. Using trees, boulders, tent poles, and/or twigs, tightly secure both sides of the tarp at a 45- to 60-degree angle to the ground.

Lean-to
A lean-to is most often used in the warm temperate and snow environments. The first four steps are basically the same as those for constructing a natural lean-to.

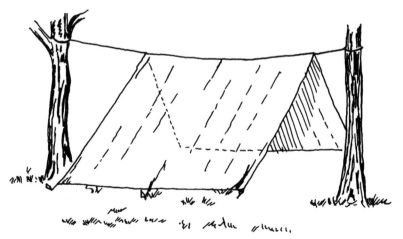

Tarp A-tent

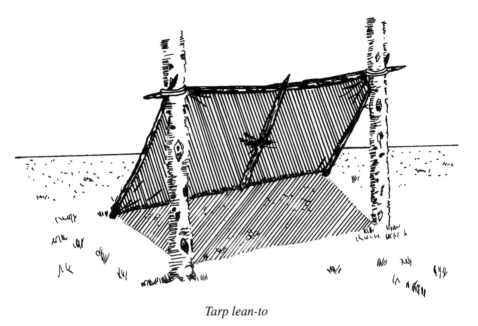

Tarp lean-to

1. Find two trees about 7 feet apart with forked branches 4 to 5 feet high on the trunk.
2. Break away any other branches that pose a safety threat or interfere with the construction of your lean-to.
3. Place a ridge pole (a fallen tree that is approximately 10 feet long and the diameter of your wrist) into the forked branches. *Note:* If unable to find two trees with forked branches, lash the ridge pole to the trees. Another option is to tie a line tightly between the two trees and use it in the same fashion as you would the pole.
4. Lay three or more support poles across the ridge pole at a 45- to 60-degree angle to the ground. Support poles need to be about 10 feet long and placed 1 to 2 feet apart. If using a line instead of the ridge pole, you may elect not to use support poles.
5. Drape the tarp over the support poles and attach the top to the ridge pole.

6. Using trees, boulders, tent poles, and/or twigs, tightly secure the tarp over the support poles and to the ground.
7. If desired, you can draw the excess tarp underneath the shelter to provide a ground cloth on which to sleep.

A-frame

An A-frame is most often used in the warm temperate and snow environments. The first three steps are the same as those for constructing a natural A-frame.

1. Find a tree with a forked branch 3 to 4 feet high on the trunk.
2. Break away any other branches that pose a safety threat or interfere with the construction of your A-frame.
3. Place a ridge pole (a fallen tree 12 to 15 feet long and the diameter of your wrist) into the forked branch, forming a 30-degree angle between the pole and the ground. *Note:* If unable to find a tree with a forked branch, lash the ridge pole to the tree. Another option is to locate a fallen tree that's at an approximately 30-degree angle to the ground, or to lay a strong ridge pole against a 3- to 4-foot-high stump.
4. Drape the tarp over the pole.
5. Using trees, boulders, tent poles, and/or twigs, tightly secure both sides of the tarp at a 45- to 60-degree angle to the ground.

Tarp A-frame

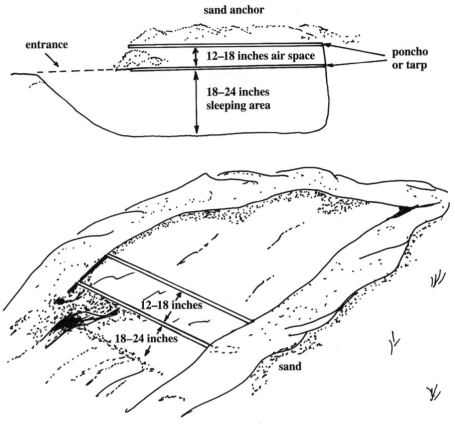

Desert/shade shelter

Desert/shade shelter

A desert/shade shelter is most often used in dry environments. It will reduce midday heat by as much as 30 to 40°. To avoid sweating and/or dehydration, build this shelter during the morning or evening hours. Until then, get out of the heat by attaching a tarp to an elevated rock or sand dune, stretching it out, and securing the other side to the ground.

1. Ideally, locate an area between rocks or dunes that has an 18- to 24-inch depression. Another option is to dig an 18- to 24-inch-deep trench that is large enough for you to comfortably lie down in.

Steve Davenport stands by a natural lean-to that was constructed from poles, branches, and boughs.

2. If a trench is dug, pile the removed sand around three of the four sides. (To provide for an adequate entryway, remove additional sand from the remaining open area.)
3. Cover the trench with your tarp (or poncho), and secure it in place by weighing down its edges with sand and/or rocks.
4. If you have another tarp (or poncho), place it 12 to 18 inches above the first. (Layering the material reduces the inside temperature even more.)

Tent
• Advantages: a tent is a very light shelter that provides excellent protection from the elements and the environment.
• Disadvantages: expensive and not always available.

BEDDING

A bed is necessary to protect you from the cold, hard ground. If a commercial sleeping pad is unavailable, bedding may be prepared using natural materials such as dry leaves, grasses, ferns, boughs, dry moss, or cattail down. For optimal insulation from the ground, the bed should have a loft of at least 18 inches. *Note:* The use of natural bedding materials is recommended *only* in actual survival situations.

FIRE

PURPOSES OF FIRE

The purposes of fire include providing light, warmth, and comfort; a source of heat for cooking, purifying water, and drying clothing; and a means of signaling.

BUILDING A FIRE

A fire is the third line of personal protection. The ability to build a fire may mean the difference between life and death. Learn how before departing for the wilderness. This section will develop the separate components of firecraft (site selection and preparation, fuel, platform and brace, heat sources, and firelays), ending with step-by-step instructions on how to build a fire. *Note:* In many wilderness areas, fires are not permitted and should be built only when emergency situations exist.

Site Selection

Look for the following when choosing a site for the fire:
- Close proximity to fire materials.
- Adequate protection from the elements (wind, rain, etc.).
- Near shelter (but not so close as to threaten the shelter).
- Flat, level ground.

Site Preparation

1. Clear a 3-foot fire circle (scrape away all leaves, brush, etc.).
2. If in a snowy or arctic environment, it may be necessary to create a platform on which to build your fire. This will prevent the snow from putting the fire out (see the section on platforms below).

A fire wall will help you make better use of the fire's heat.

3. Consider building a fire wall to reflect the fire's heat in the direction you want. One foot behind the fire circle, secure two poles into the ground. (Each pole should be approximately 3 feet high.) In order to pound the poles into the ground, you'll need to sharpen the ends and use a rock or another sturdy pole to drive them into the dirt. Next, place two more poles of similar size 4 to 6 inches in front of the others. Gather enough green logs, of wrist diameter, so that when placed between the poles they form a 3-foot-high wall. For best results, slightly lean the poles forward.

The Three Stages of Fuel

Tinder
Tinder is any material that will light from a spark. It's extremely valuable in getting the larger stages of fuel lit. There are two types of tinder: natural and man-made.

Natural tinder

Examples of natural tinder include dry or pitch wood scrapings; birch or cedar bark; straw; and dead grasses, ferns, or fungi.

For a natural tinder to work, it needs to have three characteristics: it must be dry; it needs to have edges that will light from a spark; and it must be a material that will allow oxygen to circulate within it (a necessity to keep the flame alive). In order to meet these criteria, it may be necessary to prepare the tinder prior to using it, as follows:

1. Remove any bark or pith.
2. If the tinder is moist, dry it in the sun or by placing the material between your layers of clothing (this will allow your body heat to dry the tinder as you go about your daily routine).
3. Prepare the tinder after all other firecraft requirements have been met—in other words, just before lighting the fire. If you prepare it early, it'll collect moisture from the air and may be rendered useless.

Layered forms of tinder should be prepared by working them between your hands and fingers until they're light and airy (at this point you should be able to light it from a spark).

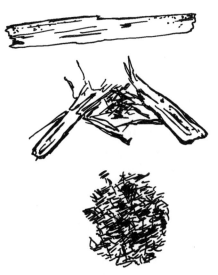

Layered tinders should be broken down until they are light and airy.

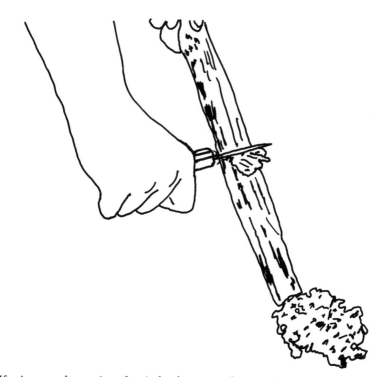

If using wood scrapings for tinder, be sure to have at least a handful prior to lighting the fire.

Wood scrapings are created by repeatedly running your knife blade, at a 90-degree angle, across a flat section of pitch or heartwood. For the scrapings to be effective as tinder, you'll need enough to fill the palm of your hand. *Note:* The best way to tell if a natural tinder will work is to try it!

Man-made tinder

There are numerous kinds of tinder available at outdoor retail stores. Fire ribbon and hexamine tablets are just two examples. They are all good. Pick the one that best meets your needs, and become familiar with how to use it.

In addition, excellent tinders can be made from petroleum jelly and cotton balls or from cotton cloth for later use. Soaking cotton balls in petroleum jelly creates a highly flammable combination that is easily lit by a spark. Charred cloth is made by placing several 2-inch squares of cotton cloth inside a tin can, which is then put under a fire's coals for fifteen to thirty minutes. For proper ventilation, the can should have several holes punched into its top. The charred cloth is easily lit from a spark produced by a flint and steel and can be used in the same fashion as a coal produced by the bow and drill.

Kindling
Kindling is usually composed of twigs or wood shavings that range in diameter from pencil lead to pencil thickness. It should easily light when placed on a small flame. Sources include small, dead twigs found on the dead branches at the bottom of many trees; shavings from larger pieces of dry, dead wood; pieces of heavy cardboard; and gasoline- or oil-soaked wood.

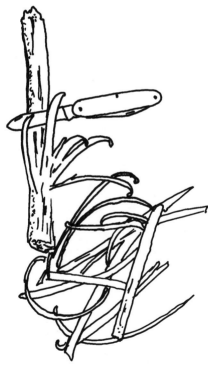

Wood shavings are easy to prepare, and their multiple edges make them an effective kindling.

Fuel
Fuel is any material that is thumb-size or bigger that will burn slowly and steadily once lit. Kinds of fuel include dry standing wood and branches; heartwood (the dry inside portion of a fallen tree trunk or large branches); green wood that is finely split; dry grasses twisted into bunches; and dry animal dung. *Note:* Use live trees only in emergency survival situations.

Platform and Brace

Platform
A platform ensures that your tinder and small kindling will not contact the moist ground. There are several different kinds of platforms.
1. Dry tree bark.
2. Dry, nonporous rock. *Caution:* Waterlogged rocks may explode when heated. Don't use them!
3. Snow platform made from green wood. To build this platform, use green logs that are wrist size and break or cut them into workable lengths (approximately 3 feet long). Construct a 3-foot-square platform by using

A snow platform keeps your fire dry even when the surrounding snow begins to melt.

When used properly, a brace and platform will keep your tinder dry and allow oxygen to circulate within it.

two rows of the green logs. Place the top row perpendicular to the bottom row.

4. Platform made in the same fashion as a snow platform, except with branches or poles from dead wood.

Brace
A brace is of vital importance. It ensures that the fire will get the oxygen it needs to exist. A branch that is of wrist thickness or a dry, nonporous rock 2 to 3 inches high will suffice. (*Caution:* Waterlogged rocks may explode when heated. Don't use them.) Lay the brace on or next to the platform. Leaning the kindling against the brace, and over the tinder, allows oxygen to circulate within the fire.

Heat Sources
Heat is required to start a fire. Without it, fuel is rendered useless. Any of the following heat sources can be used effectively: metal match, bow and drill, flint and steel, pyrotechnics, battery and steel wool, matches, and lighters.

Metal match
A metal match is effective under the harshest conditions, and it virtually never runs out. Become proficient with it, and you'll never need anything else.

Description

A metal match is made from the same material as the flint found in most cigarette lighters. It's shaped like a circular cylinder with a diameter of approximately ¼ inch and a length from 2 to 5 inches. To use a metal match:

1. Place the metal match in the center of the tinder (ensure that the tinder is on a platform and next to the brace). Hold it firmly in place, but not so firm that the tinder loses its ability to circulate oxygen.
2. Strike the metal match, with a firm yet controlled downward stroke, at a 90-degree angle with the knife blade. The resulting spark should provide enough heat to ignite the fire, but it may take several attempts to light the tinder.
3. If after five tries it has not lit, the tinder should be reworked in the palm of your hand or with a knife to ensure that adequate edges are exposed and oxygen is able to flow within it.

A metal match is an effective tool for lighting tinder, and it virtually never runs out.

Bow and drill

A bow and drill is a friction system that is effective in starting fires, but only for those who have practiced and become proficient with it. Using a bow and drill is an extremely difficult task to master. In a true survival situation, a beginner should attempt this method only if no other options are available.

Description

1. Spindle: a smooth cylinder made from a dry wood of medium hardness (such as elm, basswood, willow, cedar, yucca, aspen, or cottonwood). The spindle works best when it's about 1 inch in diameter, 8 inches long, and both ends are carved so that one is cone shaped and smooth and the other is round with rough edges.
2. Fireboard: should be made from the same wood as the spindle. (If this is impractical, then it's best to use a wood of similar hardness.) The ideal fireboard is 15 to 18 inches long, ¾ inch thick, and 3 to 5 inches wide. Carve a circular socket (three-quarters the diameter of the spindle) at least 4 inches from one end, close to the long side, and about one-quarter the thickness of the board. Next, cut a small V-shaped notch through the entire thickness of the wood. The point of the V should end at the center of the socket.
3. Cup: made from a hardwood (such as oak, hickory, or walnut). The cup should fit comfortably into the palm of your hand. Since its main purpose is to hold the spindle in place, a ½-inch-deep bowl must be carved into the center of the wood (the same diameter as your spindle).
4. Bow: a 3- to 4-foot branch of hardwood that is seasoned, stout, slightly curved, and about 1 inch in diameter. (At one end of the bow there should be a small fork.) A strong line, attached to the bow, is necessary to turn the spindle. Leather, parachute line, or even a shoelace can be used. Securely attach the line to one end of the bow. (Ideally, drill a hole through the bow, tie a knot on the line, and then run the line through the hole. The knot ensures that the line will not slip or slide forward.) Since the line's tension will inevitably loosen, use an adjustable knot to attach its free end to the fork on the other side. (If the bow doesn't have a fork, carving a notch where the adjustable knot is placed will serve the same purpose.)

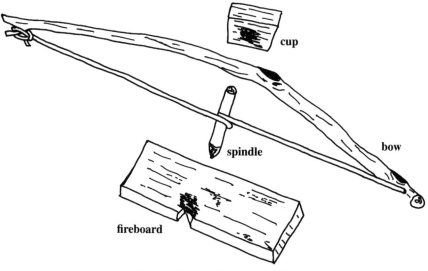

Nomenclature of bow and drill

How to use a bow and drill

1. To ensure that oxygen will circulate under the fireboard, place it on top of two sticks that are about ½ to 1 inch in diameter.

2. Set bark or another similar material between the two sticks and under the fireboard's circular socket. This not only will allow the ember (created from the friction of the bow and drill) to fall on a dry surface but also will make it easier to place it on or in the tinder.

3. To reduce friction between the cup and spindle, grease the cup socket. This can be done with animal fat, dry soap scrapings, etc. Don't use water or anything else that will create excessive moisture, since this will cause the wood to swell.

4. Twist the bow line once around the spindle so that the coned end is up and the rounded blunt end is down. If it doesn't feel like it wants to twist back out, then the bow's line needs to be tightened.

5. While holding the bow and spindle together, kneel on your right knee and place your left foot on the fireboard.

6. Insert the cone end of the spindle inside the cup, and place the round, blunt end into the fireboard socket. Holding the bow in the right hand

(at the far end) and the cup in the left, apply gentle downward pressure on the spindle (the spindle should be perpendicular to the ground). For added support and stability, rest the left arm and elbow around and upon the left knee and shin. (If left-handed, put the bow in your left hand, the cup in the right, and kneel on your left knee instead of the right.)

7. With a straightened arm, begin moving the bow back and forth with a slow, even, steady stroke. Once the fireboard and spindle begin to smoke, increase both the speed of your stroke and the amount of downward pressure on the spindle. (Don't press too hard, or you'll put the ember out.) Continue until the smoke is thick and a fair amount of dust can be seen below the fireboard's notch.

Proper posture and technique for using a bow and drill

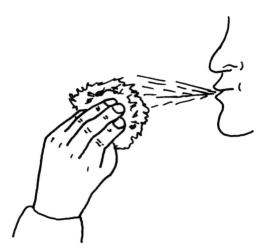

Once the coal created from the bow and drill is dropped into the tinder, gently blow on it until it lights.

8. Gently remove the spindle and push a stick or knife through the fireboard notch. (Doing so will free up any residual ember that may be stuck in the wood.)
9. Remove the bark, and carefully place the ember into the center of the tinder. Work the tinder around the ember and gently blow on it until it starts. (For best results, use lichen and manipulate it into a bird's nest shape. Drop the ember into the center of the nest, and then roll the lichen around it. Hold the nest in your hand and gently blow on it until it flames up. Be careful not to get burned.)
10. Place the tinder on your platform, next to the brace, and build the fire using the various stages of fuel that you already have prepared.

Flint and steel
This is an effective method for starting fires, but the necessary materials may be hard to find.

Description
• Flint: a fine, hard quartz. If flint is unavailable, quartzite, iron pyrite, agate, or jasper will also work.

• Steel: any piece of steel will work, but most people use the back of a knife blade.

To use a flint and steel, hold the flint in the left hand and as close to the tinder as possible. With the steel in the right hand, strike downward onto the flint. (If left-handed, hold the flint in the right hand and the steel in the left.) Direct the resulting sparks into the center of the tinder. (For best results, use cattail down and/or charred cloth as your tinder.)

Pyrotechnics
Flares should be used only as a last resort in starting fires. It's best to save these signaling devices for their intended use. However, if unable to start a fire and the risk of hypothermia is present, a flare is a very effective heat source. Its use is simple: after preparing the tinder, ignite it by lighting the flare and directing its flames onto the tinder (refer to chapter 3 for the proper use of flares). Time will be of the essence, so prepare your firelay in advance, making sure to leave an opening that's large enough to direct the flare's flame onto the underlying tinder.

Battery and steel wool
Stretching a fine grade of steel wool between the positive and negative posts of a battery will result in the igniting of the steel wool.

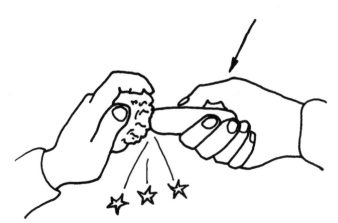

A flint and steel work best when used with a charred cloth or cattail down.

Matches

Matches run out, get wet, and seem to never work in a time of crisis. Nevertheless, they're a very good tool for starting a fire. In order to protect the match from going out, light it between cupped hands while your body blocks the flame from wind or rain. Carry matches in a waterproof container or use the waterproof variety.

Lighters

Lighters are a form of flint and steel with an added fuel source that keeps the flame going. Like matches, they also have a tendency to fail when used during inclement weather. To use, simply place the flame directly onto the tinder.

Burning glass

A convex-shaped piece of glass, such as that from binoculars, a broken bottle, or a telescope, can be used to ignite tinder by focusing the sun's rays into a concentrated source of heat.

Firelays

Once the fire has developed and you're burning the smaller stages of your fuel (thumb size), it's time to construct a firelay. Although there are many different firelays, only the tepee and pyramid fires will be covered here. All survival needs can be met with either of these methods.

Tepee fire

The tepee fire provides a concentrated heat source and is optimal for cooking purposes. Construct by laying fuel-size wood around a small flame in a tepee fashion, until the fire is strong and self-sustaining. This firelay is ideal when fuel is scarce and weather conditions aren't severe.

Pyramid fire

The pyramid fire provides light, heat, and a large bed of coals for cooking. Lay rows of fuel on top of one another, with each added row running perpendicular to the preceding one. This firelay is ideal under both mild and severe weather conditions but may not be optimal when wood is scarce.

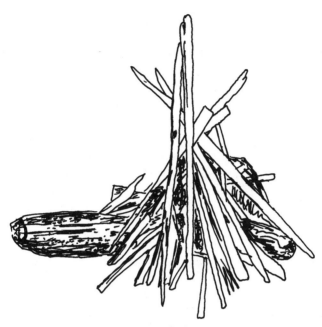

Tepee firelay

Pyramid firelay

Summary: Building a Fire
1. Select a site.
2. Prepare the site.
3. Construct a reflector (if time and materials are available).
4. Gather your materials: tinder, kindling, and fuel.
5. Gather a platform and brace.
6. Place the platform in the center of the fire circle. Place the brace either on or next to the platform.
7. Break down all the fuel so that it's in stages ranging from thumb size to larger. Place it in neat piles close to the fire circle.
8. Prepare your kindling by breaking the small twigs from larger branches or carving shavings from the larger pieces of wood. The pieces should be pencil lead to pencil thickness. Lay the kindling in neat piles close to the fire circle.
9. Prepare the tinder by breaking it down until it is fluffy, has edges, and is dry. Prepare it last to ensure that it doesn't collect moisture from the air. Keep it in a dry place until you are ready to light the fire.
10. Place the tinder on the platform next to the brace.
11. Light the tinder.
12. Once the tinder is well lit, place a handful of kindling against the brace and over the flame.

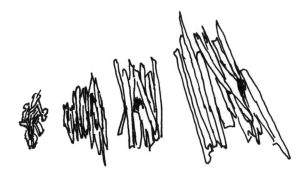

Staging the sizes of your fuel will increase your chances of success with starting a fire.

This tepee fire was built using the various stages of tinder, kindling, and fuel. Notice how the fuel has been separated into several different sizes.

13. Continue adding kindling until the flames are strong enough to add the smaller fuel. Place each additional handful perpendicular to the preceding one.
14. Finally, add the fuel in whatever manner is necessary to create the desired firelay.

Note: Store all additional firewood under a shelter or tree to keep it dry and protected from the elements. If the wood is wet, dry it out next to the fire.

BANKING THE FIRE

By banking a fire, you can preserve its embers for use at a later time. To be successful, you'll need to establish a good bed of coals. Once accomplished, cover the coals lightly with ashes and/or dry dirt. If done properly, the fire's embers will still be smoldering in the morning. To rekindle the fire, remove the dry dirt, lay tinder on the coals, and gently blow on it until the tinder ignites. When leaving, make sure your fire is completely out.

CUTTING TOOLS

Cutting tools are extremely important in the process of building a fire. With a knife and/or small wire saw, most fuels can be broken into the different stages necessary to start and maintain a fire. The care and use of these cutting tools are covered below.

Knives

General rules of using a knife

A knife has many uses and is probably one of the most versatile tools a survivor can carry. However, using a knife isn't without risk. The potential for injury is high, and every precaution should be taken to reduce this risk. Cutting away from yourself and maintaining a sharp knife, which is easier to control than a dull one, will substantially reduce your potential for injury.

Sharpening techniques

Push and pull

In a slicing fashion, repeatedly push and pull the knife's blade across a flat sharpening stone (if a commercial sharpening stone isn't available, use a flat, gray sandstone). For best results, start with the base of the blade on the long edge of the stone, and pull it across the length of the stone so that when you're done its tip has reached the center of the stone. To obtain an even angle, push the other side of the blade across the stone in the same manner. Each side should be done the same number of times.

Circular

In a circular fashion, repeatedly move the knife's blade across a circular sharpening stone or gray sandstone. Starting with the base of the blade at the edge of the stone, move the knife in a circular pattern across the stone. To obtain an even angle, turn the blade over and do the same on the other side. Each side should be done the same number of times.

To establish the best sharpening angle, lay the knife blade flat onto the sharpening stone and raise the back of the blade up until the distance between it and the stone is equal to the thickness of the blade's back side.

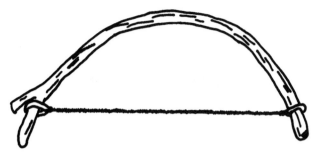

Improvised wire saws are valuable tools for cutting big pieces of fuel into smaller, more workable sizes.

Wire Saw

Wire saws are effective tools for cutting wood and should be carried in most survival kits. With very little effort, a stable cutting device can be improvised by simply attaching the saw to a green sapling. To accomplish this, bend the sapling into a half circle and secure the wire saw to each end. Once the sapling is released, there will be enough tension on the saw to make it an effective cutting device.

3

Signaling

A properly utilized signal increases a survivor's chances of being rescued. Since seconds can be the difference between life and death, don't delay in preparing or establishing a signal.

SIGNAL LOCATION

An effective signal must be utilized at an appropriate time and location. For best results, use the following guidelines when selecting a proper signaling site.

1. The site should be close to your camp or shelter.
2. It should be located in the largest available clearing.
   - If practical, the site should have 360-degree visibility.
   - If no clearing is available, placing the signal next to a stream is a good alternative.
3. Avoid shadows and overhangs that will obscure the signal.

TYPES OF SIGNALS AND HOW TO USE THEM

All of the following signals need to be used or constructed at an appropriate signaling site to be effective.

MANUFACTURED SIGNALING DEVICES

Cellular Phones/Electronic Signals

It's not uncommon for the modern backcountry traveler to carry a cellular phone as an emergency signaling device. Although a very effective signaling tool, it's not without its shortcomings.

- The phone's transmission may be lost if the survivor is in a valley or drainage. For best results, transmit from a high, clear, unobstructed location.
- In cold climates, the batteries can become cold soaked and will not work. To avoid cold soaking, keep the batteries warm by placing them between the layers of your clothing.
- Moisture, sand, and heat can all damage an electronic device. It's of paramount importance that you protect this equipment from these threats by any means available.

A cellular phone can be an effective tool when it is used properly and its battery is charged.

Illumination and Smoke Flares

Don't wait until you need a flare to become familiar with its use. Study it before finding yourself in a survival situation. Most flares can be successfully operated by following these rules.

• If practical, prepare your flare for use in advance, taking care to keep it dry. When signaling for an air rescue, don't ignite the flare until the rescuer has been sighted approaching your direction.

• Since flares have the potential to burn you, always handle them with care and never point them toward yourself or someone else. It's best to hold them away from the body, at a 45-degree angle and pointed toward the ground. Be sure the bottom is not pointing toward your body; there have been incidents where flares have ignited out of the bottom, severely burning the operator.

Greg Davenport demonstrates the proper technique for lighting and holding a day flare.

Smoke flares are best when used on clear, calm days.

• Most day flares emit a bright orange smoke that lasts approximately twenty seconds. For best results, use these flares on calm, clear days only. If the weather is bad, chances are that the smoke will dissipate before being seen.

• Most night flares emit a bright red flame that lasts approximately twenty seconds. For best results, use these flares at night.

Signal Mirrors with Sighting Holes

On clear, sunny days, signal mirrors have been seen from as far away as 70 to 100 miles. Although it's a great signaling device, it requires practice to become proficient in its use. The following are instructions on using a commercial signal mirror.

1. Holding the signal mirror between the index finger and thumb of one hand, reflect the sunlight from the mirror onto your other hand.

2. While maintaining the sun's reflection on your free hand, bring the mirror up to eye level and look through the sighting hole. If done properly, you should see a bright white or orange spot of light in the sighting hole. This is commonly called the aim indicator, or fireball.

A signal mirror with sighting hole

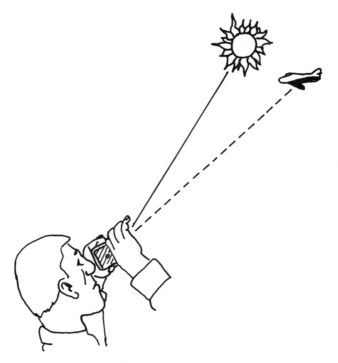

Practice using a signal mirror before its use becomes necessary.

3. Holding the mirror close to your eye, slowly turn it until the aim indicator is on your intended target. If you lose sight of the aim indicator, start over.
4. Since the mirror can be seen from great distances, sweep the horizon periodically throughout the day even if no rescue vehicles are in sight.
5. If signaling an aircraft, stop flashing the pilot after you're certain he's spotted you, as the flash may impede his vision.
6. On land, slightly wiggle the mirror to add movement to the signal.
7. At sea, hold the mirror steady to contrast the sparkles created by the natural movement of the water.

Space Blankets
These blankets have two sides, one silver and the other dark. In a snowy environment, place it in a clearing with the dark side up; otherwise, place it in a clearing with the silver side up. Weigh down the edges so it won't blow away. As you meet your other needs, a well-positioned space blanket will continue to alert potential rescuers of your location. The space blanket should be used as a signal only when not necessary to meet other survival needs.

Whistle
A whistle will never wear out, and its sound travels farther than the screams of the most desperate survivor. Always carry a whistle on your person. If

A whistle is far more effective than the loudest survivor yell.

you become lost or separated, immediately begin blowing your whistle in multiple short bursts. Repeat every three to five minutes. If rescue doesn't appear imminent, go about meeting your other survival needs, stopping periodically throughout the day to blow the whistle. It may alert rescuers of your location even if you're unaware of their presence.

IMPROVISED SIGNALING DEVICES

Fire and Smoke Signals
Using a fire and its smoke to signal rescue is similar to using a commercial illumination and/or smoke flare, except that it lasts longer.

Fire
During the night, fire is probably the most effective means of signaling available. One large fire will suffice to alert rescue to your location. Don't waste your time, energy, and wood building three fires in a distress triangle, unless rescue is uncertain. If the ground is covered with snow, build the fire on a platform (see chapter 2) to prevent the snow's moisture from putting out the fire. As with all signals, prepare the wood or other fuel for ignition prior to use.

At night a fire can be seen from several miles away.

Using various materials to change the smoke's color will make a signal fire a more effective rescue tool by creating contrasts to the existing background.

Smoke
Smoke is an effective signal if used on a clear, calm day. (If the weather is bad, chances are the smoke will dissipate too quickly to be seen.) The rules for a smoke signal are the same as those for a fire signal: you only need one; use a platform in snow environments; and prepare the materials for the signal in advance. To make the smoke contrast against its surroundings, add any of the following materials to your fire:
• To contrast with snow, create black smoke from tires, oil, fuel, etc.
• To contrast with darker backgrounds, such as green, create white smoke by adding boughs, grass, green leaves, moss, ferns, or even a small amount of water.

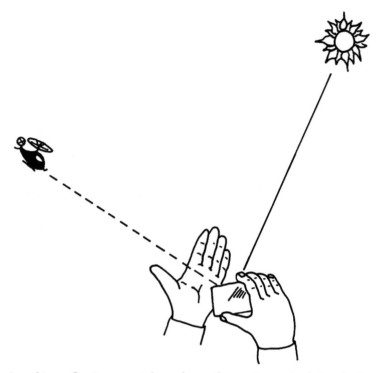

Any shiny reflective material may be used as an improvised signal mirror.

Improvised Signal Mirrors

A signal mirror can be created from anything shiny, such as a metal container, coin, credit card, watch, jewelry, or belt buckle. Although it's a great signaling device, it requires practice to become proficient in its use. The following are instructions on using an improvised signal mirror.

1. Hold the signal mirror between the index finger and thumb of one hand, and reflect the sunlight from the mirror onto the palm of your other hand.
2. Holding the reflection on your hand, create a V between your thumb and index finger.
3. Move the light reflection and your hand until the aircraft or other rescuer is in the V.

4. Move the reflected light into the V and onto your intended target.
5. Since the mirror can be seen from great distances, sweep the horizon periodically throughout the day even if no rescue vehicles are in sight.
6. If signaling an aircraft, stop flashing the pilot after you're certain he's spotted you, as the flash may impede his vision.
7. On land, slightly wiggle the mirror to add movement to the signal.
8. At sea, hold the mirror steady to contrast the sparkles created by the natural movement of the water.

Ground-to-Air Pattern Signal
A ground-to-air signal is an extremely effective device that allows you to attend to your other needs while continuing to alert potential rescuers of your location.

General rules of constructing a ground-to-air signal
• The signal should have a ratio of 6:1, with an ideal size of 18 feet long and 3 feet wide.
• Create contrast. In order to be seen from the air, a signal must stand out. An example of this would be green tree boughs on white snow.

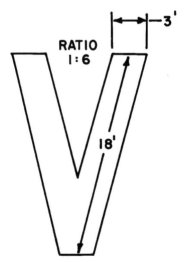

Ground-to-air signals should have a proper ratio and size when constructed.

A ground-to-air pattern signal as seen from a helicopter flying at approxi-mately 1,000 feet.

• Angularity. Because nature has no perfect lines, a signal with sharp angles will be more effective.
• Shadow. In summer, elevate the signal. In winter, stomp or dig an area around the signal that is approximately 3 feet wide. If the sun is shining, both of these methods will create a shadow, which ultimately increases the signal's size.
• Movement. Setting up a flag next to your signal may create enough movement to catch the attention of a rescue party. It is also advisable to suspend a flag high above your shelter so that it can be seen from all directions by potential rescuers.

Pattern signals and their meanings
- V: need assistance.
- X: need medical assistance.
- ↑: proceed this way.
- Y: yes.
- N: no.

Construction techniques
Each ground-to-air signal must adhere to the general rules of construction as previously outlined.

• If man-made materials are available in sufficient quantity to meet the size requirements, use them, provided they are not necessary to meet other survival needs.

• In a snow-covered clearing, form the signal by using boughs or vegetation, and stomp out a 3-foot-wide path around it.

• In a brush-covered clearing, cut out a pattern and line it with available contrasting natural materials.

• In any other situation, use your imagination to create a ground-to-air signal that meets the construction criteria.

4

Sustenance

Sustenance includes both food and water. Although food is important to replenish the body's nutrients, it's not essential in a survival situation. Water, on the other hand, is of the utmost importance. A survivor can live a month or more without food but will perish in several days without water.

WATER

WATER REQUIREMENTS

Minimum Requirements
With normal activity, an average individual needs 2 to 3 quarts of water per day. If it's extremely hot or cold or you're performing some type of hard physical activity, your need for water will increase to 4 to 6 quarts per day.

Salt Requirements
Food normally supplies adequate salt; however, salt supplements may be needed with excessive exertion and/or perspiration and are especially important for those prone to heat cramps. As a general rule, 2 grams of salt (one salt tablet) per 1 quart of water is adequate.

Effects of Dehydration
Without water, dehydration will inevitably occur. The seriousness of this condition cannot be understated. The following is a partial list of the most common symptoms of dehydration. (For further details on dehydration, refer to chapter 6.)

- Weakness.
- Decreased mental capacity.
- Dizziness.
- Decreased coordination.
- Dark yellow urine.

WATER SOURCES AND HOW TO PROCURE WATER
Surface water, precipitation, subsurface water, vegetation, and solar stills are all viable options for meeting water requirements. These sources are outlined below, along with information on recognition and procurement procedures for each.

Surface Water (Streams, Rivers, Lakes, Ponds, and Springs)
Understanding the different indicators of water will help you determine the best direction and location to look for water.
1. Terrain.
   - Rivers and streams are predominantly found in drainages.
   - Lakes and ponds are common in low-lying areas.

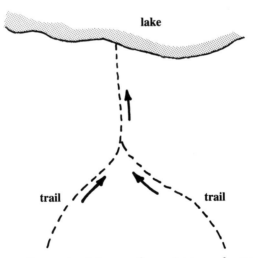

Two trails merging into one often point toward water.

This small stream was easily found in a drainage between two ridge lines. It was surrounded by several deciduous trees.

2. Vegetation.
   - Deciduous (broad-leaved) trees frequently grow next to water.
   - Abundant vegetation and/or lush grass is a good sign that water is near.
3. Mammals.
   - Two animal trails merging into one often point toward water.
   - Multiple animal droppings are a sign that water is near.
   - Most large game typically approach water at dawn and dusk.
4. Fowl.
   - Birds usually fly toward water at dawn and dusk.
   - Flocks of fowl tend to circle over water during the day.
5. Insects.
   - Insects commonly swarm around a water source.

Streams are the best source of water, since they are small and swift and tend to be less polluted. Ideally, collect the water from an area where it's moving swiftly. Avoid (unless there are no other options) areas with oily film or slicks or significant algae overgrowth.

Precipitation

Procuring rain
• Set out all available containers and improvise gutters that empty directly into them. The gutters will increase your procurement capacity and are especially helpful on days when rainfall is limited.
• In the same fashion, use the bowl that is created by a solar still (discussed below).
• After a rainfall, look in rock crevasses and fissures for accumulations of water.

Procuring snow
Don't eat ice or snow, as it reduces the body's core temperature and it takes more energy (which depletes you of vital body fluids) to break down the snow or ice than is gained from its consumption. Collect clean, fresh snow and melt it in one of the following fashions:
• In a container on a stove, next to a fire, or suspended over a fire.
• By adding it to a canteen that is partially filled with water and then agitating it. To aid in the process of melting the snow, it may become necessary to place the canteen between the layers of your clothing. (Don't place the canteen directly on your skin.)

Procuring dew
Collection of dew should occur in the early morning before it evaporates away. Dew accumulates on grass, leaves, rocks, and equipment and can be easily collected with any absorbent material. Once procured, wring it out directly into your mouth or an awaiting container.

Procuring sea ice as a water source
Old sea ice is usually salt-free and safe to drink. It is blue, brittle, and has rounded edges. New sea ice, in contrast, is gray, hard, and salty.

Subsurface Water

Beach well
A beach well is necessary when a survivor is next to an ocean shore and no fresh water is present.

1. Dig a hole away from the shoreline and beyond the first dune. (The ideal site will be surrounded by lush, green vegetation.)
2. Once water begins seeping into the hole, stop digging, and if driftwood and/or rocks are available, line the sides of the hole to prevent the sand from falling back in.
3. Allow the water to sit overnight so that the dirt and sand settle to the bottom.

Dry riverbeds
If you are without water and a dry riverbed is close by, you might consider digging for an underground water source.

1. Select a site to dig that logically has the greatest potential for water, for example, at a bend in the stream and/or where lush vegetation is present.
2. Dig a hole about 3 feet deep. If no water is seen by this depth, select another site. Once water begins seeping into the hole, dig one more foot,

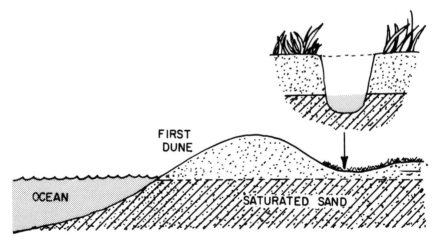

Beach well

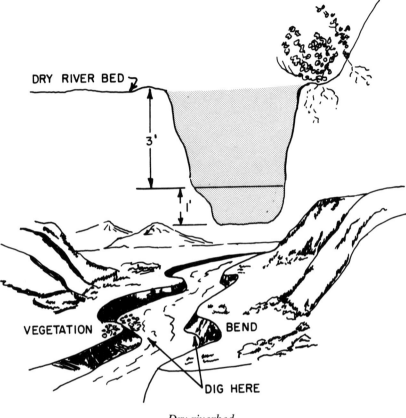

DRY RIVER BED

3'

1'

VEGETATION   BEND

DIG HERE

Dry riverbed

and then line the sides of the hole with wood and/or rocks to prevent the
dirt from falling back in.

3. Allow the water to sit overnight so that the dirt settles to the bottom.

Vegetation

Barrel cacti are prominent in the deserts of the Southwest and can provide
a limited supply of liquid. To procure it, cut off the top of a cactus (this will
be difficult without a large knife, since the cactus has a tough outer rind),
remove the inner pulp, and place it inside a porous material, such as a cotton
T-shirt. The pulp's moisture can now be easily wrung out directly into your

mouth or an awaiting container. Since the amount of fluid obtained will be minimal, don't eat the pulp. It will require more energy and body fluids to digest the pulp than can be gained from it.

Banana trees are common in the tropical rain forests and can be made into an almost unending water source by cutting them in half with a knife or machete, about 3 inches from the ground. Next, carve a bowl into the top surface of the trunk. Water will almost immediately fill the bowl, but do not drink it; the initial water will be bitter and upsetting to your stomach. Scoop the water completely out of the bowl three times before consuming.

Water vines are another source of water found in the tropical rain forests. For best results, make the top cut first, the bottom cut second, and let the water drain into your mouth or a container. Although water from most of these vines is safe to drink, avoid those that have a bitter taste or colored sap.

Note: Don't disturb native vegetation in wilderness areas unless an emergency situation exists.

Solar Stills
There are three basic techniques with which to procure water from solar heat.

Vegetation bag
To construct a vegetation bag, it is necessary to have a plastic bag and an ample supply of healthy, nonpoisonous vegetation. A 4- to 6-foot section of surgical tubing is also desirable.

1. Find a sunny slope in which to place the bag.
2. Open the plastic bag and fill it with air. Doing this makes it easier to place the vegetation inside the bag.
3. Fill the bag one-half to three-quarters full of lush green vegetation, being careful not to puncture the bag.
4. Place a small rock or similar item into the bag.
5. If you have surgical tubing, slide one end inside and toward the bottom of the bag. Tie the other end in an overhand knot.
6. Close the bag and tie it off as close to the opening as possible.
7. Place it on a sunny slope so that the opening is on the downhill side and slightly higher than the bag's lowest point.

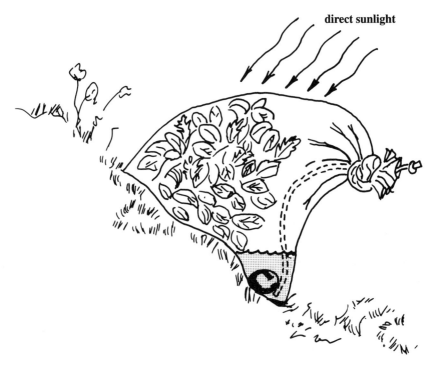

Vegetation bag

8. Position both the rock and the surgical tubing at the lowest point in the bag.
9. If using surgical tubing, simply untie the knot to drink any collected water. If no tubing is used, loosen the tie and drain off the available liquid. Be sure to drain off all liquid before sunset, or it will be reabsorbed into the vegetation.
10. For best results, change the vegetation every two to three days.

Transpiration bag

The advantage of a transpiration bag over a vegetation bag is that the same vegetation can be reused, after allowing enough time for it to rejuvenate. To construct a transpiration bag, it is necessary to have a plastic bag and an accessible, nonpoisonous shrub or tree. A 4- to 6-foot section of surgical tubing is also desirable.

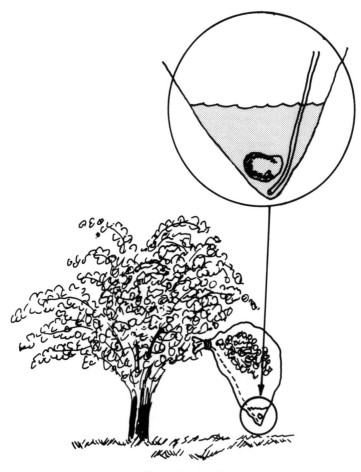

Transpiration bag

1. Find a tree or shrub that has sun exposure throughout most of the day.
2. Open the plastic bag and fill it with air. Doing this makes it easier to place the bag over the vegetation.
3. Place the bag over the lush, leafy vegetation of the tree or shrub, on the side with the greatest exposure to the sun, being careful not to puncture the bag.

4. Place a small rock or similar item into the bag's lowest point.
5. If you have surgical tubing, place one end at the bottom of the bag next to the rock. Tie the other end in an overhand knot.
6. Close the bag and tie it off as close to the opening as possible.
7. If using surgical tubing, simply untie the knot to drink any collected water. If no tubing is used, loosen the tie and drain off the available liquid. Be sure to drain off all liquid before sunset, or it will be reabsorbed into the vegetation.
8. Change the bag's location every two to three days. This will ensure optimal results and allow the previous site to rejuvenate so that it might be used again later.

Below-ground solar still
When water and vegetation are scarce, the below-ground solar still is another workable option. To construct a below-ground still, you'll need a sheet of plastic about 6 feet square and a container in which to catch the water. A 4- to 6-foot section of surgical tubing is also desirable. For best results, move the site of the solar still every two or three days.

1. Ideally, select a site that contains moisture, for example, at a bend in a dry stream, any location with lush vegetation, and/or a low-lying area where water may have collected.
2. Dig a hole approximately 3 feet across and 2 to 3 feet deep.
3. At the bottom of the hole, dig a flat-bottomed sump that is large enough for the bottom third of your container to fit in.
4. After placing the container into the sump, lay one end of the surgical tubing in it and the other end up and out of the hole. To anchor the tubing to the bottom of the container, tie a loose overhand knot at its extreme end before placing it inside. If tied loosely, the knot's weight will hold the tubing in place without impeding the flow of water.
5. Cover the hole with the plastic sheet and place a small rock onto its center, allowing it to drop 18 to 24 inches into the hole so that the lowest point is directly above the container. Secure the plastic into place with rocks and/or clumps of dirt, being especially careful that it does not come into direct contact with the dirt within the hole. (If contact occurs, condensation destined for the cup will instead be absorbed into the ground.)

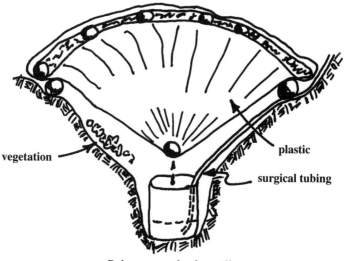

Below-ground solar still

6. Tie a knot in the free end of the surgical tubing to prevent the loss of moisture through evaporation.
7. If using surgical tubing, simply untie the knot to drink any collected water. If surgical tubing is not available, you'll need to open the still to drink the water that has been collected.
8. Ways in which to increase your water production.
   - Add nonpoisonous plants to the sides of the hole. For best results, change the vegetation every two days.
   - Recycle your urine by urinating on the ground inside the still. As the moisture from the urine evaporates, clean water is produced.
   - Pour polluted or salt water onto the ground in the still (this uses the same principle as for the urine).

WATER PREPARATION
To make water safe and more palatable, it's important to filter and purify it prior to drinking. The chances of getting a parasitic infection are extremely high if unpurified water is consumed. These infections are often accompa-

nied by vomiting, diarrhea, and dehydration, greatly reducing your ability to meet your needs.

Filtering

Filtering water does not purify it. Filtering is done to reduce sediment and make the water taste better. There are several methods of filtering water.

Seepage basin

This system is used for stagnant or swamp water. For best results, dig a hole approximately 3 feet from the swamp and to a depth that allows water to begin seeping in. Line the sides with rocks and/or wood to prevent dirt or sand from falling back into the hole. Allow the water to sit overnight so that all the sediment can settle to the bottom.

Three-tiered tripod filter

This system should be used for filtering sediment from the water. To construct it, you'll need three 7- to 8-foot-long, wrist-diameter poles, line, three 3-foot-square sections of porous cloth, grass, sand, and charcoal.

1. Build a tripod with the poles and line by laying the poles down, side by side, and lashing them together 6 inches to 1 foot from the top.
2. With the lashed end up, spread the legs of the poles out, to form a stable tripod.

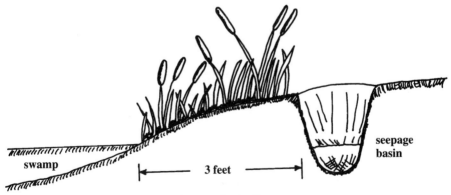

Seepage basin filter

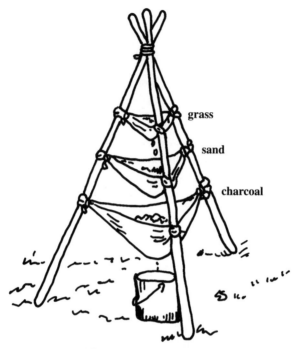

Three-tiered tripod filter

3. Tie the three sections of cloth to the tripod in a tiered fashion, and with a 6-inch to 1-foot space between each section.
4. Place grass on the top cloth, sand on the middle cloth, and charcoal on the bottom cloth.
5. To use, simply pour the water into the top section of cloth and collect it as it filters through the bottom section.

Cloth filter
Any porous material can be used to filter out sediment by simply pouring your liquid through it and into a container.

Purification
To avoid parasitic infestation, purify your water. (In a survival situation, if you are unable to treat your water, collect it from a clear, clean, fast-running creek.) There are several different methods for purifying water.

- Iodine tablets: follow the bottle's directions.
- Bleach: 2 drops to 1 quart of water. Stir and let stand for thirty minutes.
- Boil the water: rapid boil for a minimum of ten minutes.
- Commercial filtration devices.

WATER STORAGE

An ideal water container will hold a minimum of 1 quart. It should also have a wide mouth, which allows for easier filling. The best storage container, of course, is the survivor.

Improvised Water Containers

It sometimes becomes necessary to improvise containers in which to store water. You can use such things as plastic bags, cooking pots or pans, hollowed-out pieces of wood, ponchos (must use ingenuity to create a pouch), or condoms (without spermicides or lubricants). Don't limit yourself. Anything that doesn't leak can hold water.

Night Storage in Cold Environments

- Store water in a sealed container between the layers of your bedding.
- Construct a snow refrigerator.
  1. Dig a 2-foot-square section 3 feet into the side of a snowbank.
  2. Loosen the water container's caps, and place them inside the hole in an upright position.
  3. Cover the outside of the opening with a 1-foot-wide piece of snow.

WATER CONSERVATION

If water is in short supply, ration your sweat, not the water.

- Don't eat unless you have water.
- Limit your physical activity during the day. Try to accomplish any work or travel in the early and late hours of the day.
- To avoid sweating, always work and walk at an easy pace.
- Follow the principles of the COLDER acronym (covered in chapter 2).

LIQUIDS TO AVOID

Avoid drinking sea water or urine. Although both can satisfy thirst temporarily, they actually cause the body to lose additional water, ultimately resulting in further dehydration.

FOOD

NEED FOR FOOD

Although food may seem a high priority, it's not. A survivor can live many days without it. Nevertheless, the importance of food for morale and attitude cannot be overlooked. In addition, food is necessary to replenish the body's nutrients that are lost throughout the day. If water isn't available, don't eat.

FOOD SOURCES: PROCUREMENT AND PREPARATION

Vegetation

Plants are a viable food source, but unless positively identified, they can be a potentially deadly one. Four types of abundant, easily recognized, edible vegetation in the Americas are listed below. As these four sources may not always be available, an edibility test for plants and general guidelines on the edibility of berries follow.

Grass is an easily located edible plant.

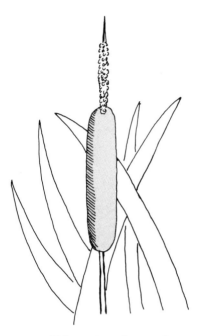

Cattails have many edible sections that can be consumed year-round.

Common edible plants
• *Grasses.* Grasses can be easily located in meadows, drainages, and dry riverbeds. The stems, roots, and leaves may be eaten raw or cooked. In addition, a good broth or tea can be made by boiling grass in water. Do not eat black or purple grass seeds. These colors indicate a fungal contamination, which if eaten could cause severe illness or death.
• *Cattails.* Cattails can be easily located in swamps, marshes, and wet low-lying areas. The cattail has a stout stem from 6 to 9 feet tall, with leaves that are light green, lean, sword shaped, and frequently higher than the flower. The flower heads are dense, brown, and cylindrical. In spring, the young shoots and flower heads are the most edible portions and are best when peeled and eaten raw or boiled. During the early summer, the flower's pollen can be eaten raw or dried and pounded into a flour for later use. In late summer, the peeled roots are another source of flour when dried and pounded into a powder.

Pine trees are a prominent food source that can be found throughout most of North America.

Common green seaweed can be easily located on both sides of the Pacific and Atlantic Oceans.

- *Pine trees.* Pine trees are prominent in many North American forests, easily identified as tall, multiple-branched trees with sçaly bark and sharp evergreen needles arranged in bundles of two, three, or five. In addition, many have large, egg-shaped cones. Pine needles may be eaten raw or cooked, or they can be boiled in water to make a broth or tea. The cambium layer, between the bark and inner wood, may be eaten raw or cooked or can be dried and pounded into a flour for later use. The seeds, located under the scales of the cones, may also be eaten raw or cooked.
- *Common green seaweed* (sea lettuce). Green seaweed can be easily located on both sides of the Pacific and Atlantic Oceans. Since seaweed found on the beach tends to be moldy, it's best to choose plants that are attached to rocks or floating free. Seaweed may be eaten raw or dried until crisp and used in soup or broth.

Bear grass is located throughout most of the northwestern United States, and like most grasses, is an abundant, easy-to-find edible plant.

Universal edibility test

If food is scarce and rescue is not imminent, you may need to eat other plants. *Important:* If unable to identify a plant, *do not* eat it without first performing the edibility test. The test takes twenty-four hours to complete, and during this time no other foods can be consumed. Because of the time element and the restrictions on your diet, this process should be undertaken only if such foods are necessary to your survival.

General rules of the edibility test

- Ensure that there's an abundant supply of the plant.
- Use only fresh vegetation.
- Always wash your plants with treated water.
- Perform the test only on one plant or plant part at a time.
- During the test, don't consume anything else other than purified water.
- Don't eat for eight hours prior to starting the test.

Identifying characteristics of plants to avoid

- Mushrooms or mushroomlike appearance.
- Umbrella-shaped flower clusters, resembling parsley, parsnip, or dill.
- Plants with milky sap or sap that turns black when exposed to the air.
- Bulbs (resemble onion or garlic).
- Carrotlike leaves, roots, or tubers.
- Bean or pealike appearance.
- Plants with fungal infection (common in plants procured off the ground).
- Plants with shiny leaves or fine hairs.

To test a plant

1. Break the plant into its basic components: leaves, stems, roots, buds, and flowers.
2. Test only one part of the potential food source at a time.
3. Smell the plant for strong or acidlike odors. If present, it may be best to select another plant.
4. Prepare the plant part in the fashion in which you intend to consume it (raw, boiled, baked, etc.).
5. Place a piece of the plant part being tested on the inside of your wrist for fifteen minutes. Monitor for burning, stinging, or irritation. If any

**Mushroom or
mushroomlike
appearance**

**Umbrella-shaped
flower clusters**

**Bulbs resembling
onion or garlic**

**Carrotlike leaves,
roots, or tubers**

**Bean- and pealike
appearance**

**Plants with shiny
leaves or fine hairs**

Six characteristics of plants to avoid

of these occur, discontinue the test, select another plant (or another component of the one being tested), and start over.

6. Hold a small portion (about a teaspoonful) of the plant to your lips and monitor for five minutes. If any burning or irritation occurs, discontinue the test, select another plant (or another component of the one being tested), and start over.

7. Place the plant on your tongue, holding it there for fifteen minutes. Do not swallow any of the plant juices. If any burning or irritation occurs,

Aggregate berries are 99 percent edible.

discontinue the test, select another plant (or another component of the one being tested), and start over.

8. Thoroughly chew the teaspoon-size portion of the plant part for fifteen minutes. Do not swallow any of the plant or its juices. If you experience a reaction, discontinue the test, select another plant (or another component of the one being tested), and start over. If there is no burning, stinging, or irritation, swallow the plant.

9. Wait eight hours. Monitor for cramps, nausea, vomiting, or other abdominal irritations. If any occur, induce vomiting and drink plenty of water. If you do experience a reaction, discontinue the test, select another plant (or another component of the one being tested), and start over.

10. If no problems are experienced, eat ½ cup of the plant, prepared in the same fashion as before. Wait another eight hours. If no ill effects occur, the plant part is edible when prepared in the same fashion as tested.

11. Test all parts of the plant you intend to use. Some plants have both edible and poisonous sections. Do not assume that a part that is edible when cooked is edible when raw (or vice versa). Always eat the plant in the same fashion in which the edibility test was performed on it.

12. After the plant is determined to be edible, eat it in moderation. Although considered safe, large amounts may cause cramps or diarrhea.

The berry rule

In general, the edibility of berries can be classified according to their color and composition. The following is a guideline (approximation) to help you determine whether a berry is poisonous. In no way should the berry rule replace the edibility test. Use it as a general guide to determine whether the edibility test needs to be performed upon the berry. The only berries that should be eaten without testing are those that you can positively identify as nonpoisonous.

- Green, yellow, and white berries are 10 percent edible.
- Red berries are 50 percent edible.
- Purple, blue, and black berries are 90 percent edible.
- Aggregate berries, such as thimbleberries, raspberries, and blackberries, are 99 percent edible.

Bugs

Many bugs are edible and easy to obtain. They are a valuable source of proteins, fats, and vitamins and shouldn't be overlooked. Six edible bugs are listed below, followed by general characteristics of poisonous bugs that should be avoided.

Edible bugs

- *Grubs.* Grubs, or insect larvae, are present in rotten logs, under the bark of dead trees, under rocks, and in the ground. They may be eaten raw or cooked.

Although slugs may be eaten raw, they are far more appealing when cooked.

• *Grasshoppers.* Grasshoppers can be easily located in open fields on grass stems. For best results, collect them in the coolness of the early morning. To eat, remove the grasshoppers' legs (which are barbed and tend to get stuck in the throat) and cook the insects in any fashion desired. Since grasshoppers carry parasites, never eat them raw.

• *Ants.* Ants are present throughout most of the world and are usually found in nests on the ground. To collect enough ants to make a meal, disturb the nest with a stick, and as the ants climb onto the stick, continually dip it into a container of water. Don't stop until an adequate supply is gathered. Ants can be eaten raw or cooked. If eaten raw, however, be sure to kill the ants before putting them into your mouth, or they might bite you.

• *Slugs.* During the spring and summer, slugs are usually present in damp meadows and forests. Although they may be eaten raw, they are far more appealing when cooked.

• *Maggots.* Maggots (larvae of flies) can be easily located within decaying matter and may be eaten raw or cooked.

• *Earthworms.* Earthworms are predominantly located in moist, warm soil and may be eaten raw or cooked.

Bugs and bug characteristics to avoid
• Bugs that carry disease: flies, mosquitoes, or ticks.
• Poisonous bugs: centipedes, scorpions, or spiders.
• Bugs with fine hairs, bright colors, or eight or more legs.

Mollusks
Mollusks can be an excellent food source if you're near water, but they should be avoided from April to October. During this time, they accumulate certain poisons that can be harmful to humans.

Avoid mollusks from April to October.

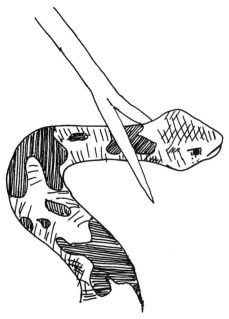

Use a long, forked stick to pin the snake's head to the ground.

Snails
Snails can be easily located in shallow, sandy or muddy water and should be steamed, boiled, or baked prior to eating. They taste best when cooked in the shell and then removed.

Mussels
Mussels are often attached to rocks along the shoreline and can be easily procured when the tide is out. Like snails, mussels may be steamed, boiled, or baked but taste best when cooked in the shell and then removed. Never eat mussels that are above the water at high tide; they will usually cause an upset stomach and vomiting.

Reptiles (Snakes)
All poisonous and nonpoisonous freshwater and land snakes are edible and can be located almost anywhere there is cover. Snakes can be cooked in any fashion, but all should be skinned and gutted. For best results, hunt for

snakes in the early morning or evening hours. Always be cautious when dealing with poisonous snakes.

Once you spot a snake, stun it by hitting it with a thrown rock or stick. Using a 6-foot stick with a fork at one end, pin the snake's head to the ground. Once it's securely trapped, kill it with a rock, knife, or another stick. Be careful!

Note: Avoid accidental poisoning by burying the head of any poisonous snakes.

Fish
Fish are commonly found in almost all sources of water. The general rules of fishing and four methods of fish procurement are outlined below.

When to fish
- Just before dawn or just after dusk.
- At night when the moon is full.
- When bad weather is imminent.

Where to fish

Oceans
- Reefs provide an abundant source of fish that can be procured most easily by using a spear.
- Tidal channels are ideal for hook and line fishing.
- Shallow water and low tides are optional for hook and line, spear, and chop fishing.

Lakes and large streams
Fish tend to be close to banks and shallow water in the morning and evening hours.

Small streams
- Calm, deep pools, especially where it transitions from ripples to calm or calm to ripples.
- Under outcroppings or overhanging undercuts, brush, or logs.
- In eddies below rocks or logs.
- At the mouth of an intersection with another stream.

Methods of fish procurement

Set lines

Attach multiple lines to low-hanging branches that will bend but not break when the fish bites. Watch to determine what the fish are feeding on and, if practical, use it as bait.

If no hooks are available, improvise using bones, safety pins, small twigs, etc. Line can be made from fishing line, parachute line inner core, small twine, or other available slender line.

Bare-handed

Catching fish bare-handed is best done in small streams with undercut banks. Place your hand into the water and slowly reach under the bank, moving it as close to the bottom as possible. Let your arm become one with the stream, moving it slightly with the current. Once contact with a fish is

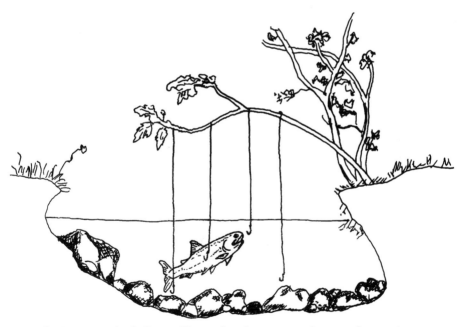

Setting out multiple lines will greatly enhance your chances of procuring a fish.

made, gently work the palm of your hand up its belly until you reach its gills. Grasp the fish firmly behind the gills, and scoop it out of the water.

Spears

To make a straight spear, procure a long, straight sapling and sharpen one end to a barbed point. If practical, fire-harden the tip to make it more durable by holding it a few inches above a bed of hot coals until it's brown.

To make a forked spear, procure a long, straight sapling and fire-harden the tip. Snugly lash a line around the stick 6 to 8 inches down from one end. Using a knife, split the wood down the center and to the lash. To keep the two halves apart, lash a small wedge between them. (For best results, secure the wedge as far down the shaft as possible.) Sharpen the two prongs into inward-pointing barbs.

For best results, use a spear in shallow water and/or where fish are visible. Because of the difference in light refraction above and below the water, it is important to place the spear tip into the water before aiming to obtain proper alignment. Next, slowly move the spear as close to the fish as possible and allow them to become accustomed to it. When ready, quickly

Fire-hardening the tip of your spear will make it far more durable.

Forked spear

spear the fish and hold it down against the bottom of the stream. Finally, reach down and grasp the spear tip firmly, pulling it and the fish out of the water.

Net

To make a net, procure a 6-foot sapling and bend the two ends together to form a circle. A forked branch can also be used by forming a circle with the forked ends. Allow some extra length for a handle. Lash the ends together. Pull an undershirt over the circle formed by the sapling. Tie the shirt's arm and neck holes closed, and secure the bottom by tying a knot on each side of the handle. *Note:* An undershirt is a source of heat conservation and protection: do not use as a net if weather conditions are prohibitive.

As with the spear, use a net in shallow water or a similar area where fish are visible. Because of the difference in light refraction above and below the water, it is important to place the net into the water before aiming to obtain proper alignment. Next, slowly move the net as close to the fish as possible and allow them to become accustomed to it. When ready, scoop the fish up and out of the water.

Chop fishing

Chop fishing is most often used to procure ocean fish at night and during low tide. Fish in shallow water are stuck and stunned with the back of a machete or other solid handheld object. The stunned fish are then easily removed from the water. *Note:* Fish are attracted to light, and shiny or reflecting objects may be used to lure them into shallower water.

How to prepare fish for consumption

To prevent spoilage, prepare the fish as soon as possible in the following fashion: Gut the fish by cutting up its abdomen and then removing the intestines and large blood vessels that lie next to the backbone. Remove the gills. When applicable, scale and/or skin the fish. Smoke, sun-dry, or cook in any fashion desirable.

When to avoid eating fish
Avoid eating fish that has any of the following characteristics.
- Bad odor.
- Suspicious color (gills should be red to pink; scales should be pronounced, not faded).
- Soft flesh that remains indented after being pressed on.
- Slimy body.

Birds

All birds are edible. If nests are near, eggs also may be available for consumption.

Birds are commonly found at the edge of the woods where clearings end and forests begin, on banks of rivers and streams, and on lakeshores and seashores.

Methods of procuring birds

Baited hook

Using a baited hook (meat works best) on fishing line is probably the best method for procuring birds. A secured fishing line is preferable to a hand-held one; it allows a survivor to attend to other tasks while waiting for a bird to take the bait.

Ojibwa bird snare

The Ojibwa snare is an effective snaring device, yet it requires time and materials to create. If you have both, it may be worthwhile to set one out.

Find a sapling that is 1 to 2 inches in diameter and cut the top off so that it's approximately 4 to 5 feet high. To prevent birds from landing on the top, carve it into a point. The bait can also be attached here. Make a hole slightly larger than $1/2$ inch in diameter near the top of the sapling. The perch will eventually be placed into this hole. Cut a stick 6 to 8 inches long and about $1/2$ inch in diameter for the perch. If you prefer, you can sharpen one end of the stick and attach the bait there.

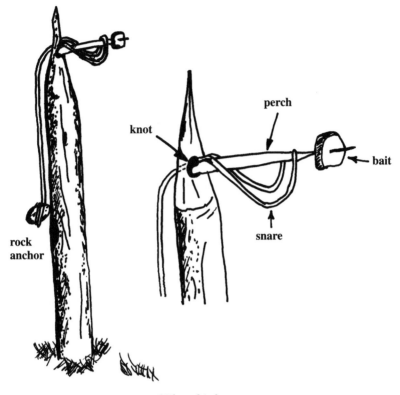

Ojibwa bird snare

Using a piece of 3- to 4-foot line, make a slip knot or noose at one end. The noose should be 6 to 8 inches in diameter. One to 2 inches beyond the noose, tie an overhand knot. (This knot is instrumental in securing the perch to the sapling until a bird lands on it.) Pull the free end of the snare line through the hole in the sapling until the knot reaches the opening. Insert the perch into the hole, and use the knot to lightly secure it in place. If using the perch to hold the bait, be sure to bait it first. Tie a rock or heavy stick to the free end of the line. It must be heavy enough to pull the noose tight once the bird dislodges the perch from the sapling. Lay the noose on top of the perch. It may be easier to tie the rock to the line before inserting the perch into the hole.

Clubbing or catching
Other options include clubbing or catching, but these methods are extremely difficult and often unsuccessful.

How to prepare birds for consumption
Pluck all birds unless they are scavengers or seabirds, which should be skinned. Leaving the skin on other kinds of birds will retain more of their nutrients when cooked. Cut off the neck close to the body. Cut open the chest and abdominal cavity and remove the insides. Save the neck, liver, and heart, which are all edible. Cook in any desired fashion. Scavenger birds should be boiled a minimum of twenty minutes to kill parasites.

Mammals
Signs of the presence of mammals are well-traveled trails, which usually lead to feeding, watering, and bedding areas; fresh tracks and droppings; and fresh bedding sign (nests, burrows, trampled down field grass).

Handheld devices for killing mammals
Skill and precise aim are required to approach and kill a mammal with any handheld killing device. Best results come with practice.

Rocks
Rocks are used to stun the animal long enough for you to approach and kill it. Hand-sized stones work best. Aiming toward the animal's head and shoulders, throw the rock as you would a baseball.

Throwing sticks
The ideal stick is 2 to 3 feet long and larger or weighted at one end. Holding the thin or lighter end of the stick, throw it in either an overhand or sidearm fashion. For best results, aim for the animal's head and shoulders.

Spears
For details on how to construct a spear, refer to the preceding section on fish. A throwing spear should be between 5 and 6 feet long. To throw a spear, hold it in your right hand, and raise it above your shoulder so that

Bola

the spear is parallel to the ground. Be sure to position your hand at the spear's center point of balance. (If left-handed, reverse these instructions.) Place your body so that your left foot is forward and your trunk is perpendicular to the target. In addition, point your left arm and hand toward the animal to help guide you when throwing the spear. Once positioned, thrust your right arm forward, releasing the spear at the moment that will best enable you to strike the animal in the chest or heart.

Bola
A bola is a throwing device that immobilizes small game long enough for you to approach and kill it.

To construct a bola, use an overhand knot and tie three 2-foot-long lines together 3 to 6 inches from one end. Securely attach rocks (each about ½ pound) to the other end of the three lines.

To use a bola, hold the knot in your hand, and twirl the line and rocks above your head or to one side until adequate control and speed are obtained. Once this is accomplished, release the knot when the bola is directed toward the intended target.

Weighted club

This device not only can be used to kill an animal at close range but is also a valuable tool for meeting other survival needs.

To construct a weighted club, find a rock that is 6 to 8 inches long, 3 to 4 inches wide, and approximately 1 inch thick. Cut a 2- to 3-foot branch of straight-grained wood that is approximately 1 to 2 inches in diameter. Hardwood is best, but softwood will also work. Six to 8 inches down from one end of the stick, snugly lash a line around the wood. Split the wood down the center and to the lash with a knife. (You can also use a strong forked branch and secure the rock between the two forked branches.) Insert the stone between the wood and as close to the lashing as possible. Finally, secure the rock to the stick with a tight lashing above, below, and across the rocks.

Use a weighted club in the same fashion as a throwing stick.

Weighted club

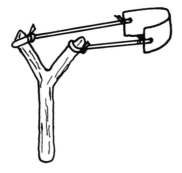

Improvised slingshots are effective weapons for procuring small game.

Improvised slingshot

This is a fairly effective tool for killing small animals. Elastic cord, bungee cord, or surgical tubing are required for its construction. In addition, you need webbing or leather to make a pouch.

To construct a slingshot, cut a strong forked branch with a base 6 to 8 inches long and forked sides of 3 to 5 inches. Carve a notch around the top of each forked side, ½ inch down from the top. Cut two 10- to 12-inch pieces of elastic cord or line, and secure them to the branches by wrapping the end of each cord around the carved notches and then tightly lashing them together.

Cut a piece of webbing or leather 3 inches long and 1 to 2 inches wide. Make a small hole that is centered and ½ inch in from each side. Using the free end of each elastic cord, run ½ inch through the hole in the webbing or leather. Secure the cord to the webbing or leather by lashing it together.

To use a slingshot, hold a small marble-size rock in the slingshot's pouch between the thumb and index finger of your right hand. Place your body so that your left foot is forward and your trunk is perpendicular to the target. Holding the slingshot with a straightened left arm, draw the pouch back toward your right eye. Position the animal between the forked branches and aim for the head and shoulder region. Release the rock.

Snares and traps

Snares and traps are highly advantageous because they allow you to meet your other survival needs while still attempting to procure food.

Method of catching animals with a snare or trap
- Strangle: the animal is caught with a snare that tightens around its neck.
- Mangle: the animal is killed when the snare's trigger is tripped and a log or other device falls on it. Some snares also force the animal into spears when hit by the log.
- Hold: usually a hole or box that holds the animal in place.

Snare placement
When placing the snare, avoid disturbing the area as much as possible. Avoid removing the bark from any natural material used in the snare's construction. If the bark is removed, camouflage the exposed wood by rubbing dirt on it. Since animals avoid humans, it's important to remove your scent from the snare. One method of hiding your scent is to hold the snaring material over smoke or underwater for several minutes prior to its final placement. If establishing a snare on a well-traveled trail, try to utilize the natural funneling of any surrounding vegetation. If natural funneling isn't available, create your own with strategically placed sticks. (Again, hide your scent.)

The snare's loop (discussed below) should be situated so that its height is equal to the height of the animal's head. Secure the snare in place by using one of the triggers discussed below. Place multiple snares at burrow openings and on well-traveled trails in the area.

Snare or trap triggers
1. Two-pin toggle. The two-pin toggle trigger is primarily used to procure small game in a strangling snare.

    To construct a two-pin toggle, procure two small forked or hooked branches that ideally fit together when the hooks are placed in opposing positions. If unable to find two small forked or hooked branches, construct them by carving notches into two small pieces of wood until they fit together.

    To use a two-pin toggle, firmly secure one branch into the ground with the fork pointing down. Attach the snare to the second forked

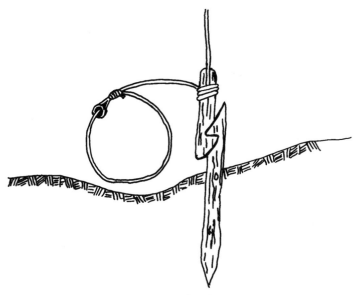

Two-pin toggle trigger

branch, which is also tied to a twig or other device so that when the trigger is tripped, the animal is captured or strangled. To arm the snare, simply bend the twig and attach the two-pin toggle together. The resulting tension will hold it in place.

2. Figure H. The figure H trigger is also used to procure small game in a strangling-style snare. If this trigger is used properly, it will work regardless of which way the animal approaches the snare.

To construct a figure H, procure two sticks that are 18 inches long and 1 inch in diameter and one stick that is 8 to 10 inches long and 1 inch in diameter. Notch the two longer sticks approximately 1 inch from the top. Make the notch the same width as the diameter of the shorter stick. Notch the shorter stick, on opposing sides, ½ to 1 inch from its ends. These notches should be the same width as the diameter of the longer sticks.

To use a figure H, pound the two longer sticks into the ground with their carved notches on the up side but in opposing directions. Be sure

Figure-H trigger

the notches are the same height from the ground. Place the shorter piece so that its grooves fit into the longer stick's notches. Attach the snare to the shorter stick, which is also tied to a twig or other device so that when the trigger is tripped the animal is captured or strangled.

3. Figure four. The figure four is usually used to hold logs in a mangle-type snare or trap.

To construct a figure four, procure two sticks that are 12 inches long and 1 inch in diameter and one stick that is 4 to 6 inches long and 1 inch in diameter. Notch the first long stick 2 inches from one end and cut it at a 45-degree angle at the other. In addition to being at opposite ends, the notch and 45-degree angle must also be on opposite sides of the stick.

In the second long stick, carve a notch approximately 1 inch from one end and 2 inches from the other. Here the two notches need to be on the same side of the stick and slightly angled away from the center of the stick. Sharpen the end where the notch is 2 inches in to a point so that it can be used to hold bait when the snare is completed. Carve the short stick so that both ends have 45-degree angles, with the angles on the same side of the stick.

To use a figure four, attach the first long stick to a tree so that the notch is up and the end with a 45-degree angle is down. Be sure that the notch points out and the long end of the angled side is away from the tree. Place the second long stick onto the first so that the notch and pointed end are up. It is held in place when the short piece is placed between the two long sticks, forming a figure four. The entire structure is held in place by the tension that occurs when the short piece is attached to a line, which ideally loops over a sturdy branch and is secured to a suspended log or other heavy object. This object will fall and mangle an animal that trips the trigger.

Types of snares and traps
1. Twitch-up strangle snare.

An animal caught in this type of snare will either strangle itself or be held securely until your arrival. To construct a twitch-up strangle snare, begin by constructing a simple loop snare. Using snare wire that's strong enough to hold the mammal you intend to catch, make a fixed loop at one end. To do this, bend the wire 2 inches from the end,

Figure-four trigger

fold it back on itself, and twist or wrap the end of the wire and its body together, being sure to leave a small loop. Twist the fixed loop at its midpoint until it forms a figure eight. Fold the top half of the figure eight down onto the lower half.

Run the free end of the wire through the fixed loop. The size of the snare will determine the resultant circle's diameter. It should be slightly larger than the head size of the animal you intend to catch. If in extremely cold weather, it's best to double the wire to prevent the snare from breaking.

To finish the strangle snare, find a sapling that when bent to 90 degrees is directly over the snare site you have selected. Using a two-pin toggle, securely insert the longer forked branch into the ground at the snare site, and with its hook pointing downward. Attach the free end of the snare wire, created earlier, to the other forked branch. (*Note:* A figure H can also be used as a trigger for this snare.) With a short piece of snare wire, secure the free branch to the sapling, bend the sapling down, and attach the trigger together. The resulting tension will hold the trigger in

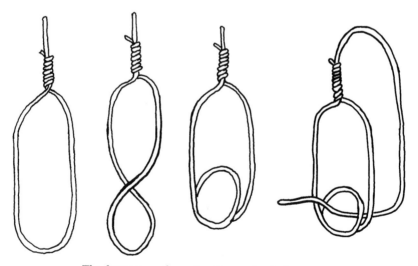

The four steps of constructing a simple loop snare

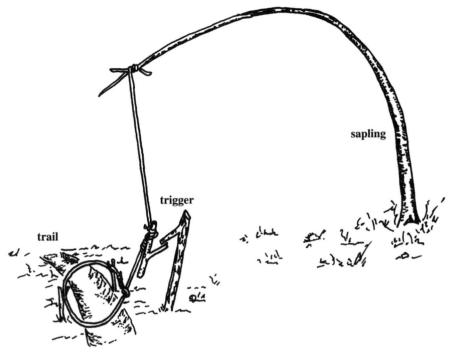

Twitch-up strangle snare

place. Adjust the snare height to the approximate position of the animal's head. When an animal places its head through the snare and trips the trigger, it will be snapped upward and strangled by the snare. *Note:* It may be necessary to place two small sticks into the ground to hold the snare in place on the trail.

2. Squirrel pole.

A squirrel pole is an efficient means by which to catch multiple squirrels with minimal time, effort, or materials. Attach several simple loop snares (page 102) to a pole approximately 6 feet long, then lean the pole onto an area with multiple squirrel feeding sign (look for mounds of pinecone scales, usually on a stump or fallen tree). The squirrel will inevitably use the pole to try to get to his favorite feeding site.

A squirrel pole is an efficient means by which multiple squirrels can be caught with minimal time, effort, or materials.

3. Canadian ace mangle snare.

An animal caught in this snare will be mangled and killed. It's used primarily on larger predatory game, such as coyotes. To construct a Canadian ace mangle snare, set up a figure-four trigger, as outlined above, approximately 2 to 3 feet high on a small 1- to 2-foot-wide tree. Gather multiple straight, sturdy branches of various lengths, and sharpen both ends. Securely stick the branches side by side around the figure four, with the shortest ones in front. Place bait (preferably meat) on the sharpened figure-four stick.

Attach line to the center section of the figure four, run it up and over a strong branch in the tree, and tie it 1 foot from the upside end of a heavy, well-positioned log. The log should be 6 to 8 feet long and form a 25- to 30-degree angle between its high side, its low side, and the ground. When an animal tries to eat the meat, it will set off the trigger, and the upper end of the log will fall and drive its head and shoulders into the sharpened sticks.

4. Box trap.

   A box trap is ideal for small game and birds. It keeps the animal alive, thus avoiding the problem of having the meat spoil before it's needed for consumption. To construct a box trap, assemble a box from wood and line, using whatever means are available. Be sure it's big enough to hold the game you intend to catch. Create a two-pin toggle (see above) by carving L-shaped notches in the center of each stick. For the two-pin toggle to work with this trap, it's necessary to whittle both ends until they're flat. Be sure the sticks you use are long enough to create the height necessary for the animal or bird to get into the box. Take time to make a trigger that fits well. Set the box at the intended snare site.

Canadian ace mangle snare

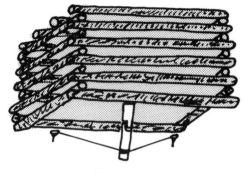

Box trap

Secure two sticks at opposite ends, on the outside of one of the box's sides. Tie a line to each stick, bring the lines under the box, and secure them to the middle of the lower section of your two-pin toggle. Connect the two-pin toggle together, and use it to raise the side of the box that is opposite the two stakes. Adjust the lines until they're tight and approximately 1 inch above the ground. Bait the trap. When an animal or bird trips the line, it'll be trapped in the snare.

Skinning, gutting, and butchering an animal
Before skinning an animal, be sure it is dead. Once you're sure, cut the animal's throat and collect the blood in a container for later use (add to stews, boil down to a paste, etc.). If time is not an issue, wait thirty minutes before starting to skin. This allows the body to cool, which in turn makes it easier to skin and also provides enough time for most parasites to leave the animal's hide.

Skinning an animal

Small game
Make a cut along the animal's back and pull the hide, at the cut, in opposing directions until removed. This method destroys most of the hide and should be used only on the smallest of animals.

Large game

A larger animal can be hung from a tree by its hind legs or skinned while lying on the ground. If musk glands are present, remove them. (Musk glands are usually found at the bend between the upper and lower parts of the hind legs.) Free the hide from the animal's genitals by cutting a circular area around them, then make an incision that runs just under its hide and all the way up to the neck. Avoid cutting the entrails. Next, cut around the joint of each extremity. From there, extend the cut down the inside of each leg until it reaches the midline incision.

At this point, the hide can be removed. On smaller animals, it will pull off with little effort. On larger game, you'll need to use your knife to loosen the hide from the body (avoid cutting through the entrails or the hide). If skinning on the ground, use the hide to protect the meat; don't remove it until after gutting the animal. Be sure to save the hide, since it can be tanned

Skinning small game

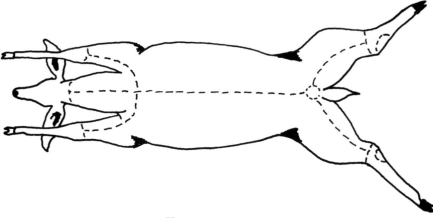

Skinning large game

and with a little effort made into clothing or other tools of survival (covered in chapter 2).

Gutting an animal

Place the carcass, belly up, on a slope or hang it from a tree by its hind legs. Make a small incision just in front of the anus, and insert your index and middle fingers into the cut, spreading them apart to form a V. Slide the knife into the incision and between the V formed by your two fingers. Use your fingers to push the internal organs down (away from the knife) and as a guide for the knife as you cut up the abdominal cavity to the breastbone (avoid cutting the bladder or other internal organs). Cut around the anus and sex organs so that they will be easily removed with the entrails. If the bladder or other internal organs are punctured, wash the meat as soon as possible.

Remove the entrails, pulling them down and away from the carcass. Save the liver and kidneys for later consumption. (If the liver is spotted, a sign of disease, discard all internal organs and thoroughly cook the meat.) Cut through the diaphragm and reach inside the chest cavity until you can touch the windpipe. Cut or pull the windpipe free and remove the chest cavity contents. Save the lungs and heart for later consumption. (All internal organs can be cooked in any fashion but are best when used in a stew.) At this point, finish skinning the animal.

Butchering an animal
If you intend to eat the liver, you'll need to remove the small black sac (gallbladder), as it's not edible. If it breaks, wash the liver immediately to avoid tainting the meat. Since fat spoils quickly, it should be cut away from the meat and promptly used (best in soups). Small game is easily butchered by cutting the legs, back, and breast sections free of one another. When butchering large game, cut it into meal-size roasts and steaks that can be stored for later use. Cut the rest of the meat along the grain into long, thin strips about ⅛ inch thick, to be preserved by smoking or sun drying (covered later in this chapter). Don't forget to skin the head; the meat, tongue, eyes, and brain are all edible, as is the marrow inside bones. Keep the bones, brain, sinew, hooves, and other parts. Each will serve many different survival needs.

METHODS OF COOKING FOOD
When possible, cook all food to ensure that parasites and bacteria are killed.

Boiling
Boiling is the best method, since all the vital nutrients of the food product can be obtained by consuming the broth. If no container is available, it may be necessary to improvise one. You might use a rock with a bowl-shaped center (*warning:* avoid rocks with a high moisture content, as they may explode) or a thick, hollowed-out piece of wood that can be suspended over the fire.

Frying
Place a flat rock on or next to the fire (*warning:* avoid rocks with a high moisture content, as they may explode). Let it get hot, and use it in the same fashion as you would a frying pan.

Broiling
Broiling is ideal for cooking small game over hot coals. Before cooking the animal, sear its flesh with the flames from the fire. This will help keep

the juices, containing vital nutrients, inside the animal. Next, run a non-poisonous skewer (a branch that is small, straight, and strong) along the underside of the animal's backbone. Finally, suspend the animal over the coals, using any means available.

FOOD PRESERVATION

1. If able, keep all animals alive until ready to consume.
2. In winter, freeze the meat in meal-size portions to avoid unnecessary spoilage from constant thawing and freezing.
3. Construct a refrigerator in one of the following ways.
   - Bury the food in a snow refrigerator (covered earlier in this chapter).
   - Wrap the food inside a waterproof container and securely place it in a stream.
   - Dig a 2-foot hole in a moist, shady location. Wrap your food in a waterproof container, surround it with vegetation, and place it inside the pit. Cover the food with sticks and dirt until the hole is filled.
4. Cook all your food as soon as it is obtained, and when you are ready to use it, recook it to kill any bacteria or parasites. Monitor closely for spoilage. If spoiled, use for bait.
5. Dry meat in one of the following ways.
   - Sun drying. Use the long, thin strips of meat you cut when butchering the animal. Hang the meat in the sun out of animals' reach. To do this, run snare wire or line between two trees. If using snare wire, skewer the line through the top of each piece of meat before attaching it to the second tree. If using other line, hang it first and then drape the strips of meat over it. For best results, the meat should not touch its other side or another piece.
   - Smoking. Use the long, thin strips of meat you cut when butchering the animal. Construct a smoker and use it as follows:
     1. Build a 6-foot-tall tripod (covered under water filtration and purification, above.)
     2. Attach snare wire or line around the three poles, in a tiered fashion, and so that the lowest point is at least 2 feet above the ground.
     3. If using snare wire, skewer the line through the top of each strip of meat before extending it around the inside of the next pole. If

Sun-drying meat is an effective method of preserving it.

using other line, hang it first and then drape the strips of meat over it. For best results, the meat should not touch its other side or another piece.

4. Cover the outer aspect of the tripod with any available material, such as a poncho. Avoid contact between the outer covering and the meat. For proper ventilation, leave a small opening at the top of the tripod.

5. Gather an armload of green deciduous wood, such as willow or aspen, and prepare it by either breaking the branches into smaller pieces or cutting the bigger pieces into chips.

6. Build a fire next to the tripod, and once a good bed of coals develops, transfer them to the ground in the center of the smoker. Continue transferring coals as needed.

7. To smoke the meat, place small pieces or chips of green wood on the hot coals. Once the green wood begins to heat up, smoke should occur. Keep adding chips until the meat is dark and brittle—about twenty-four to forty-eight hours. At this point, it is done.

Note: Since an actual fire would destroy the smoking process, monitor the wood to ensure that it doesn't flame up. If it does, put it out, but try to avoid disrupting the bed of coals too much.

FOOD STORAGE
• Don't store any food in your shelter, as it will attract animals.
• Put all food inside a container or cover it during the day to avoid insect infestation.

A smoker is a quick, efficient method of meat preservation.

Using a tree cache at night will help protect your food against bears and rodents.

• To avoid bear and rodent problems, hang your food in a tree cache at night. For best results, hang it as high as possible and as far from the trunk as practical.

EMERGENCY FOOD
It is advisable to carry a one-day supply of food that is high in fats and complex carbohydrates and requires no cooking. Examples are energy bars or meat bars, nuts, and dehydrated fruits or vegetables.

5

Travel and Navigation

As long as you are able to meet your survival needs, stay put. Rescue attempts are far more successful when searching for a stationary survivor. However, there are three situations when travel from your present location to another might be considered.

1. If your present location doesn't have adequate resources to meet your needs (e.g., for personal protection, sustenance, signaling).
2. If rescue doesn't appear to be imminent.
3. If you know your location and have the navigational skills to travel to safety.

TOOLS OF NAVIGATION

A map and compass are the basic tools that most backcountry travelers use when navigating in the wilderness. A review of how to use them is outlined below, along with information on other methods of navigating.

MAP NOMENCLATURE

The particulars of any map's nomenclature can usually be found within its main body and the surrounding margins. For a map to be an effective tool, however, you must become familiar with the one you're using before departing for the wilderness, as there are several different types of maps available. The basic components of most commercial maps are as follows.

Scale and Series

Scale

A scaled map represents the ratio of the map to real life. The following are commonly used scales:

- 1:24,000 scale: every inch on the map represents 24,000 inches of natural terrain.
- 1:64,000 scale: every inch on the map represents 64,000 inches of natural terrain.

Series

A series map represents the relationship of the map to the amount of latitude and longitude that is displayed (covered below). The following are commonly used series:

- 15 minute series: map covers 15 minutes of latitude and 15 minutes of longitude.
- 7.5 minute series: map covers 7.5 minutes of latitude and 7.5 minutes of longitude. (It would take four of these maps to cover the same surface area as one 15 minute series map.)

Even when traveling on a trail, Bob Milks, a USAF survival instructor, has the foresight to carry a map and compass.

Colors and Symbols

The colors and symbols on a map denote different things and are very useful in evaluating the terrain. The most common colors and their meanings are as follows:

- Green: woodland.
- White: nonforested, nonwater areas, such as rocks or meadows.
- Blue: water.
- Black: man-made structures, such as buildings or trails.
- Red: prominent man-made features, such as major roads.
- Brown: contour lines (covered below).

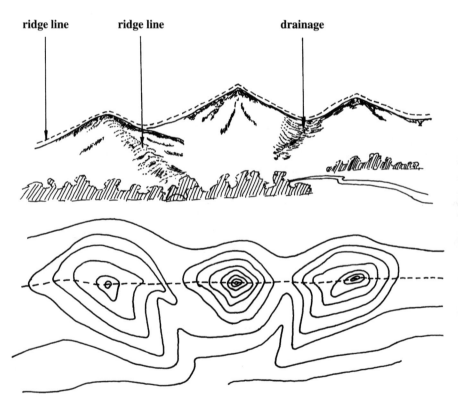

Contour lines are two-dimensional representations of the existing three-dimensional terrain.

MN

Magnetic variation allows you to adjust for the difference between true north and magnetic north.

Contour Lines

Contour lines are imaginary lines, superimposed on a topographic map, that connect points of equal elevation. The contour line interval, usually found in the map's margin, is the distance between two contour lines. The actual distance varies from one map to the next. The following is a basic guide on how to interpret the lay of the land as shown by a map's contour lines:

- Steep terrain: lines will be close together.
- Gradual elevation gains and losses: lines are relatively far apart.
- Drainage: lines will form a V pointing toward higher elevation.
- Ridge lines: lines will form a V pointing away from higher elevation.
- Peaks: lines forming a closed circle

Magnetic Variation

The magnetic variation is usually listed on the bottom of a topographic map. An arrow labeled "MN" indicates magnetic north; a second line, with a star at the end, is true north. Maps are set up for true north. This variation, commonly called declination, is valuable in compensating for the difference between true north and magnetic north (compass heading). The purpose of this information will be discussed in more detail later.

Latitude and Longitude Lines

There are imaginary lines that encircle the globe, creating a crisscross grid system. These lines help you identify your location.

Latitude lines

• These are east-west-running lines numbered from 0 to 90 degrees north and south of the equator.

• The 0-degree latitude line runs around the globe at the equator, and from there the numbers rise north 90 degrees and south 90 degrees. In other words, the equator is 0 degrees latitude, the North Pole is 90 degrees north latitude, and the South Pole is 90 degrees south latitude.

• Latitude is noted at the extreme ends of the horizontal map edges.

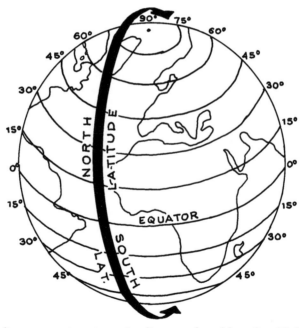

Latitude lines are east-west-running lines numbered from 0 to 90 degrees north and south of the equator.

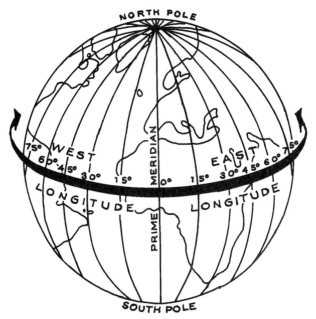

Longitude lines are north-south-running lines numbered from 0 to 180 degrees east and west of Greenwich, England (prime meridian).

Longitude lines
• These are north-south-running lines numbered from 0 to 180 degrees east and west of Greenwich, England, the line commonly referred to as the prime meridian.
• The longitude lines begin at 0 (Greenwich, England), traveling east and west until they meet at the 180th meridian, which is often referred to as the international dateline. The 0 meridian becomes the 180th meridian once it intersects the extreme north and south sections of the globe.
• Longitude is noted at the extreme ends of the vertical map edges.

Rules for reading latitude and longitude
Both latitude and longitude lines are measured in degrees (°), minutes ('), and seconds ("). There are 60 minutes between each degree and 60 seconds between each minute. For example, 45° 30' and 30".

It is also important to distinguish north from south when defining your latitude, and east from west for longitude.

• Latitude. For the example given above, if north of the equator, your latitude would read 45 degrees, 30 minutes, and 30 seconds north; if south of the equator, 45 degrees, 30 minutes, and 30 seconds south latitude. *Note:* A latitude line will never be over 90 degrees north or south.

• Longitude. If east of the prime meridian, your longitude would read, for example, 120 degrees, 30 minutes, and 30 seconds east longitude; if west of the prime meridian, 120 degrees, 30 minutes, and 30 seconds west longitude. *Note:* A longitude line will never be over 180 degrees east or west.

Whenever giving a latitude and longitude intersection, always read the latitude first.

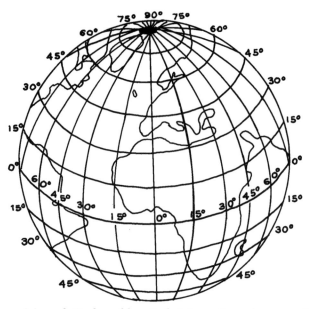

Whenever giving a latitude and longitude intersection, always read the latitude first.

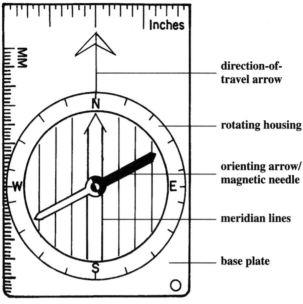

Orienteering compass nomenclature

COMPASS NOMENCLATURE

This section covers the nomenclature of an orienteering compass and compasses of similar structure. These compasses have a circular housing mounted on a rectangular base. Further details are outlined below.

Rectangular Base Plate

The sides of the base plate have millimeter and inch markings. These markings are used to relate a map measurement to that of a relative field distance. The front has a direction-of-travel arrow. The arrow is parallel to the long edge and perpendicular to the short edge. Compass headings are read from the point where the bottom of the direction-of-travel arrow touches the numbers on the edge of the circular compass housing. The direction-of-travel arrow must always point toward the intended destination when a heading is being taken.

Circular Housing

A circular rotating housing sits on the base plate. Its outer ring has the four cardinal points (N, S, E, W) and degree lines starting at north and numbered clockwise to 360 degrees. The bottom of the housing has an etched orienting arrow that points toward the north marking on the outer ring.

Magnetic Needle

The compass needle sits beneath the glass of the circular housing. It floats freely, and one end, usually red, points toward magnetic north (not true north). Magnetic north lies near Prince of Wales Island in northern Canada. Observe below how the magnetic variance affects readings done in the United States.

Notice the line that passes through the Great Lakes and along the coast of Florida. This line is an agonic line, which has no variation. In other

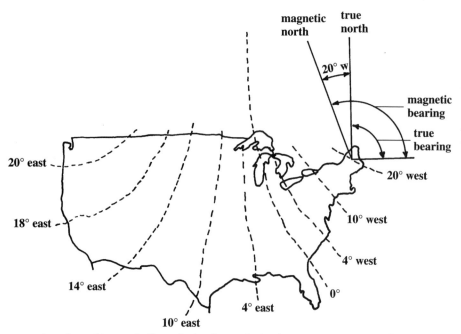

Agonic and isogonic lines depict the variation between magnetic and true north.

words, a compass heading of 0 or 360 degrees would point toward both magnetic and true north.

The other lines, which are isogonic lines, have variations from true north. The line that extends through Oregon has a variation of 20 degrees east. Note that when this line is extended, the compass bearing of 360 is 20 degrees to the east of true north. The opposite would be true for the line extending through Maine. In this case, a compass bearing of 360 would be 20 degrees west of true north. Because of these variations, adjustments must be made in order to use a map and compass together (covered below).

Note: If you hold the compass close to a metal object, the needle will be drawn toward it.

USING A MAP AND COMPASS TOGETHER

DETERMINE GENERAL LOCATION
Anytime you're traveling in the wilderness, you should maintain a constant awareness of your general location. Through this awareness, you can better pinpoint your location by orienting the map and triangulating (below).

ORIENTING THE MAP WITH A COMPASS
Orienting the map aligns its features to those of the surrounding terrain. This process is extremely helpful in determining your specific location.
1. Get to high ground. This will help you evaluate the terrain once the map is oriented.
2. Open the map and place it on a flat, level surface. If possible, protect it from the dirt and moisture with something such as a poncho.
3. Rotate the circular housing on the compass until the bottom of the direction-of-travel arrow is touching the true north heading (when doing this, you *must* account for the area's given declination, as outlined below).

   Declination is the difference between magnetic north (MN) and true north (★). True north is represented on a map, and magnetic north is a compass heading. (In other words, a 360-degree map heading—true north—is not necessarily a 360-degree compass heading.) This variation is usually depicted on the bottom of most topographic maps. Examples of both east and west variations are as follows:

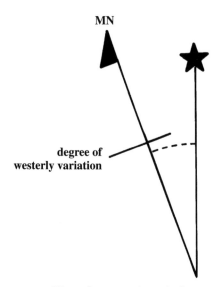

MN

degree of
westerly variation

Westerly magnetic variation

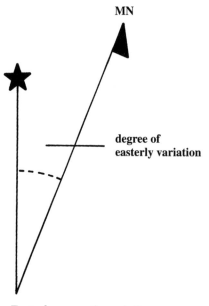

MN

degree of
easterly variation

Easterly magnetic variation

- West variation. If magnetic north is located west of true north, which is the case for most of the eastern United States, you would add your declination to 360 degrees. The resultant bearing would be the compass heading equivalent to true north at that location.
- East variation. If magnetic north is located east of true north, which is the case for most of the western United States, you would subtract your declination from 360 degrees. The resultant bearing would be the compass heading equivalent to true north at that location.

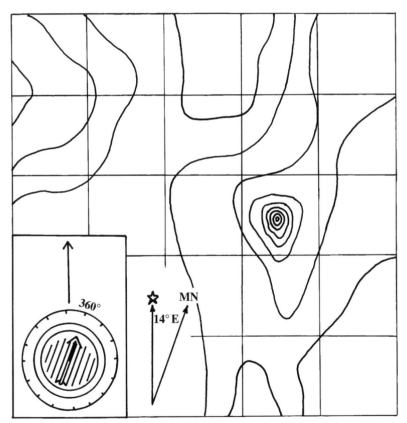

Be sure to account for the magnetic variation when orienting the map with a compass.

4. Set the compass on the map with the edge of the long side resting next to (parallel to) the north-south margins (longitude line). Be sure that the direction-of-travel arrow is pointing toward the north end of the map.
5. Holding the compass in place, rotate the map until the floating magnetic needle is inside the etched orienting arrow of the base plate (red portion of the needle forward). This is called boxing the needle.
6. Double-check to ensure that the compass is still set for the variation adjustment, and if correct, weigh down the map edges to keep it in place.
7. At this point, the map is oriented to the lay of the land, and the map features should reflect those of the surrounding terrain.

TRIANGULATING TO PINPOINT YOUR LOCATION
Triangulating is a process of identifying your specific location. For best results, get to high ground with 360 degrees of visibility.
1. Orient the map as outlined above.
2. Positively identify three of the surrounding landmarks, ideally 120 degrees apart, on your map by using the following guidelines.
   - Contour: evaluate the landmark's contour, translating it into a two-dimensional appearance, and search for a matching contour outline on your map (see map nomenclature section above).
   - Distance: determine the distance from your present position to the landmark to be identified. This may be calculated as follows:
        From 1 to 3 kilometers, you should be able to see the individual branches of each tree. From 3 to 5 kilometers, you should be able to see each individual tree. From 5 to 8 kilometers, the trees will look like a green plush carpet. At greater than 8 kilometers, not only will the trees appear like a green plush carpet, but there will also be a bluish tint to the horizon.
   - Elevation: determine the landmark's height as compared with that of your location.
3. Using your compass, point the direction-of-travel arrow at one of the identified landmarks, and then turn the compass's housing until the etched orienting arrow boxes the magnetic needle (red end forward). At the point where the direction-of-travel arrow intersects the compass housing, read and record the magnetic bearing. Repeat this process for the other two landmarks.
4. Before working further with the map, ensure that it's still oriented.

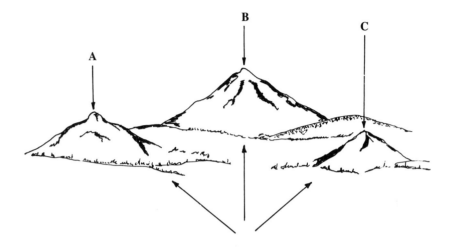

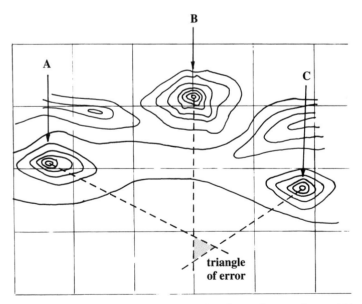

When triangulating, your position should be located somewhere within or around the triangle of error.

5. Place the front left tip of the long edge of the compass on the identified map landmark, and while keeping the tip in place, rotate the compass until the magnetic needle is boxed (red end forward). Double-check that your compass heading is correct for the landmark being used.

6. Lightly pencil a line from the landmark down, following the left edge of the compass base plate. You may need to extend the line. Repeat this process for the other two landmarks. Each time, ensure that the map is still oriented.

7. Ultimately, a triangle will form where the three lines intersect, and your position should be located within or around the triangle.

8. For final position determination, evaluate the surrounding terrain and how it relates to the triangle displayed on the map.

DETERMINING AND MAINTAINING A FIELD BEARING

ESTABLISHING A FIELD BEARING

Never travel unless you know both your present position and where you intend to go.

Establishing a Field Bearing with a Map and Compass

1. Orient your map to the lay of the land.

2. Lightly draw a pencil line from your present location to your intended destination.

3. Place the top left edge of the compass on your intended destination.

4. Rotate the compass until the left edge is directly on and parallel to the line you drew.

5. Next, rotate the compass housing—keeping the base of the compass stationary—until the floating magnetic needle is boxed inside the orienting arrow (red portion of the needle forward).

6. Read the compass heading at the point where the bottom of the direction-of-travel arrow touches the numbers of the circular compass housing. This heading is the field bearing to your intended destination.

Establishing a Field Bearing with Only a Compass

1. Hold the compass level, and point the direction-of-travel arrow directly at the intended destination site.

2. Holding the compass in place, turn its housing until the magnetic needle is boxed directly over and inside the orienting arrow (red portion of the needle forward).

3. Read the heading at the point where the bottom of the direction-of-travel arrow touches the numbers of the circular housing. This heading is the field bearing to your intended destination.

Deliberate Offset

If your destination is on a road, consider a heading with a deliberate offset. In other words, use a field heading several degrees to one side of your final location. Since it is very difficult to be precise in wilderness travel, this offset will help you in deciding to turn left or right once you intersect the road.

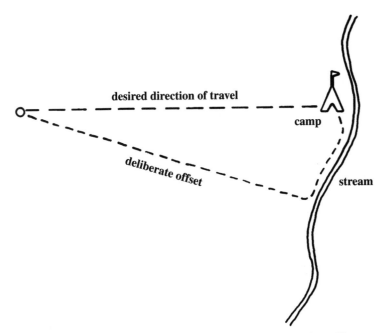

Using a deliberate offset is a useful tool when traveling in the wilderness.

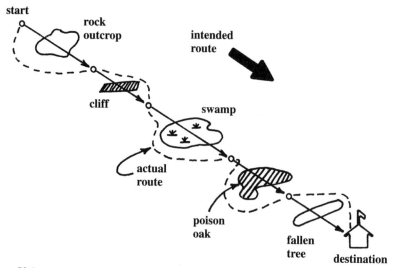

Using point-to-point navigation allows you to steer clear of obstacles.

STAYING ON ROUTE DURING TRAVEL

Maintaining a Field Bearing
• Point-to-point: pick objects in line with your field bearing. Once one point is reached, recheck your bearing and pick another. This method allows you to steer clear of obstacles.
• Following the compass: holding the compass level, while keeping the magnetic needle boxed, walk forward in line with the direction-of-travel arrow.

Four-Point Checklist for Travel
1. Establish the compass heading (azimuth) to your desired location. Once confident of your azimuth, trust your compass and stay on your heading.
2. Determine the distance to travel and estimate the number of paces it will take to reach your final destination (a pace is measured each time the same foot hits the ground). Fairly level terrain: 650 paces to 1 kilometer. Steep terrain: paces will nearly double for each kilometer.
3. Create checkpoints. When traveling, be aware of each major terrain feature en route. Determine how many paces it takes to each, marking them

off as they are passed. By doing this, you'll maintain a constant awareness of your location during the trek.
4. Estimate your arrival time. This will help you set realistic goals on the
distance to travel each day.

DETERMINING DIRECTION WITHOUT A COMPASS

If, for some unforeseen reason, you're lost and without a compass, it's still
possible to identify each of the cardinal directions. With this information,
you can orient a map and determine your location. Several methods are
outlined below.

USING CONSTELLATIONS TO DETERMINE DIRECTION

North of the Equator
Polaris (the North Star) can be found if the Big Dipper or Cassiopeia is
visible. (Polaris is approximately due north, and most constellations appear
to rotate around it.) When both constellations are seen, the North Star can

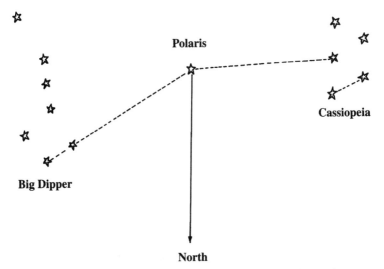

*In the Northern Hemisphere, the Big Dipper and Cassiopeia can be
utilized to find the northern cardinal direction.*

be located approximately halfway between them. If both can't be seen, Polaris may be found in one of the following ways:

• The Big Dipper is a formation of stars that resembles a ladle with the opening of the cup facing toward Polaris. At the forward tip of the Big Dipper, there are two stars. A line drawn (from the back end toward the opening) that connects them together will point toward the North Star. Extend the line four to five lengths beyond the second star to find Polaris.

• Cassiopeia is made from five stars that form a W, with the opening always facing toward Polaris. The central star of Cassiopeia's W points toward the North Star. A line extended about four to five lengths (one length is equal to the distance between any two of Cassiopeia's stars) from this central point will locate Polaris.

South of the Equator

Although there is no southern star, approximate due south can be determined if you can identify the Southern Cross and Pointer Stars. The Southern Cross is a formation of four stars in the pattern of a cross. The Pointer Stars are simply two stars side by side.

The southern cardinal direction can be found by using these constellations together. Create a straight line from the top to the bottom of the Southern Cross, and extend it toward the ground. Draw a perpendicular line from the middle of the Pointer Stars. At the point where the two lines intersect, create a third one that extends straight down. This line represents the southern cardinal direction.

If the Pointer Stars aren't visible, you can find the southern cardinal direction from the Southern Cross. Using the distance between the top and bottom stars of the Southern Cross, create a line that extends out from the bottom star five times this distance. At the point where the line ends, draw a second line straight down toward the ground. This line represents a southern direction.

USING A STICK AND SHADOW
TO DETERMINE DIRECTION

The shadow method is the same both north and south of the equator. However, it's advisable to use this method only between 26.4 degrees and 66.5 degrees latitude in either hemisphere. At greater than 66.5 degrees latitude,

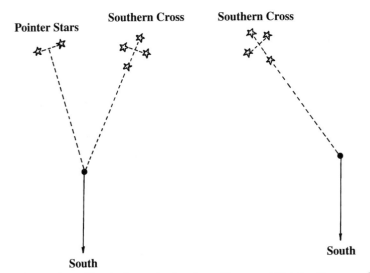

In the Southern Hemisphere, the Southern Cross and Pointer Stars can be utilized to find the southern cardinal direction.

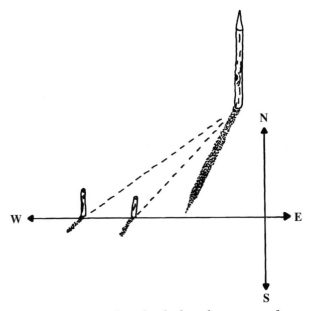

When using a stick and shadow, the shadow always moves from west to east.

During a trip to the Colville National Forest, the stick and shadow pictured were used to orient a topographical map to the lay of the land.

the sun's position above the horizon makes this method ineffective. Between 26.4 degrees south latitude and 24.6 degrees north latitude, the sun can be north or south, depending on the time of year. Unless you are aware of the sun's position for the time of year, it may be difficult to identify north from south.

1. Pound a stick vertically into the ground at a location that's fairly level. To make a crisper shadow, carve a point at the top of the stick.
2. Clean the surrounding ground of debris and vegetation.
3. Lay a rock or small stick at the end of the shadow, or push a small twig into the ground.
4. Mark the shadow's tip approximately every five minutes (the more marks, the greater the accuracy).
5. Draw a straight line in the dirt between each rock or stick.
6. Since the shadow progresses from west to east, the first marking on the line is west and the second is east. (The sun rises in the east and sets in the west, so its resulting shadows will always run from west to east.)

7. Draw a perpendicular line through the east-west line to determine north and south. If in the Northern Hemisphere, the shadow tip side is north; if in the Southern Hemisphere, the shadow tip side is south.

USING A WATCH TO DETERMINE DIRECTION

Using a watch is a gross method of determining the cardinal directions, but in a pinch, it will suffice.

North of the Equator

1. Point the watch's hour hand toward the sun.
2. Holding the watch in this position, draw an imaginary line midway between the hour hand and 12 o'clock. (If in daylight savings time, use the 1 o'clock symbol instead.)

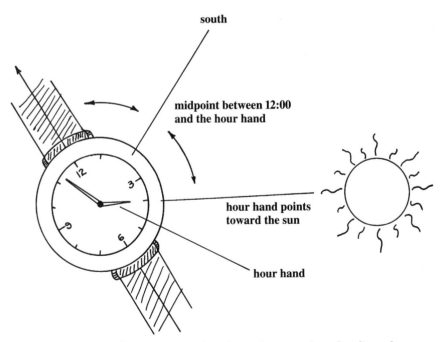

Proper technique for using a watch to determine a southern heading when north of the equator

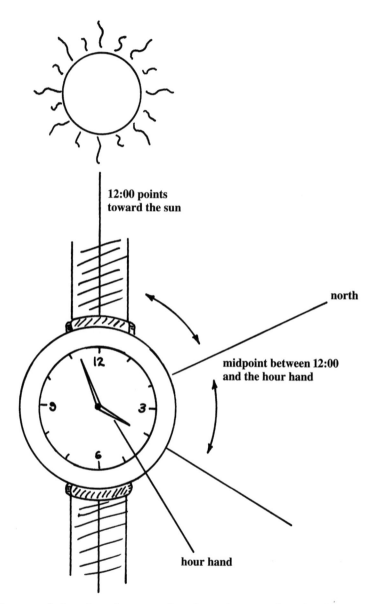

12:00 points
toward the sun

north

midpoint between 12:00
and the hour hand

12

9   3

6

hour hand

*Proper technique for using a watch to determine a northern heading when
south of the equator*

3. This imaginary line is an approximate southern heading. Another line drawn perpendicular to this one makes it possible to determine north, east, and west.

South of the Equator

1. Point the watch's 12 o'clock symbol toward the sun.
2. Holding the watch in this position, draw an imaginary line midway between the hour hand and 12 o'clock. (If in daylight savings time, use the 1 o'clock symbol instead.)
3. This imaginary line is an approximate northern heading. Another line drawn perpendicular to this one makes it possible to determine south, east, and west.

ADDITIONAL INFORMATION ON TRAVEL

ENERGY CONSERVATION
- Maintain a constant steady pace to avoid overheating and/or exhaustion.
- Take frequent rest breaks throughout the day.
- When walking uphill, use a rest step, which is done by locking the knee with each step. This process takes the weight off the muscle, allowing it to rest, and places it on the skeletal system.
- Keep your clothing loose and layered to avoid energy loss through overheating.

TERRAIN CONSIDERATIONS
- When trails are available, use them, provided they are in line with your direction of travel.
- For uphill travel, stand straight, shorten steps, and use the rest step.
- For downhill travel, keep the knees slightly bent and walk with slow, small, controlled steps.
- Talus travel (big rocks) is easy uphill but may create a problem when going down. If, when traveling downhill, you feel your footing giving way, move quickly to the next rock.
- Scree travel (small rocks) is easy descending; ascending is difficult, since the rocks give way. Shuffling your feet or using a plunge step will make scree travel much easier.

- Contouring—hiking at a constant elevation around a valley—will expend less energy than traveling straight through it (down and up).
- Avoid travel in the desert or deep snow unless absolutely necessary.
- For river crossings, select a safe site. Always undo the waist belt on your pack before crossing so that you can quickly remove your pack if you fall.

LEAVING WORD

- If you are lost, stay put. If you must move on, leave word for rescue.
- Leave a note listing your time of departure, route, and intended destination.
- Mark your trail by tying flags to branches, breaking branches, etc.

PACKING YOUR GEAR FOR EASE OF TRAVEL

A well-balanced pack will add to the comfort and safety of the survivor. Ideally, load the heaviest part of the pack at the top, centered as close to the body as possible. On rough or steep terrain, it is advisable to lower the center of gravity for improved stability and balance.

If a pack is not available, constructing a bedroll to carry gear is a good option. Lay a poncho or other large square piece of waterproof material flat on the ground. Place all gear on the edge of the material. Pad any sharp or hard items. Roll the material over the gear and continue until all the material is used. Tie the resulting roll at each end and every 12 inches in between with available line or rope. Finally, tie both ends securely together and slide the roll over your head and onto either shoulder.

6

Health

Survival medicine is simply first aid and CPR with a twist. Ultimately, the environment and the amount of time before you return to civilization may have the biggest impact upon any health issues that arise. The weather may be bad and the nearest medical facility may be miles from your location. It's highly advisable that you receive adequate first aid and CPR training, and in no way should you consider this chapter a replacement for that instruction.

GENERAL HEALTH ISSUES

Your ability to fend off injury and infection plays a significant role in how well you handle any given survival situation. Proper hydration, nutrition, hygiene, and rest all affect your ability to ward off problems that occur in the wilderness.

STAYING HYDRATED

Without water, you'll die in about three to five days. In addition, dehydration will directly affect your ability to make logical decisions about how to handle any given problem.

Ways in Which Fluids Are Lost
- In cold environments, the body loses fluids during the process of warming itself.
- By sweating due to either heat or intense activity.
- Through urination and defecation.

**Signs and Symptoms of Dehydration
(Each Level Builds on the Previous One)**

Mild
- Excessive thirst.
- Irritability.
- Weakness and nausea.

Moderate
- Dizziness.
- Headache.
- Difficulty walking.
- Tingling sensation in the limbs.

Severe
- Dim vision.
- Painful urination.
- Swollen tongue.
- Deafness.
- Numbness of skin.

Treatment of Dehydration
The best treatment is prevention. This can be accomplished by drinking a minimum of 2 to 3 quarts of water a day, more if you are hot or exerting a lot of energy. If symptoms do occur, decrease your activity and drink enough potable water to get your urine output up to at least 1 quart in a twenty-four-hour period. *Don't* drink seawater or urine, since they're of no benefit and will only worsen your dehydrated state.

NOURISHMENT
Nourishing foods boost morale, provide valuable energy, and replace lost nutrients (salt, vitamins, etc.). Food is not as much of a necessity as water, however, and you may be able to go without it for several weeks.

CLEANLINESS
Staying clean not only improves morale, but it also helps prevent infection and disease. The following are some different methods of staying clean in the wilderness:

While climbing in northwestern Washington, Greg Davenport takes time to rest and rehydrate.

- Wash with water (creek, lake, etc.).
- Air- or sun-bathe for thirty minutes to two hours daily.
- Keep hair trimmed to decrease likelihood of parasites and disease.
- Brush teeth and stimulate gums daily. If no toothbrush is available, fray the end of a green twig and use it just like a toothbrush and/or stimulate your gums with a finger twice daily.
- Monitor and clean your feet daily. Wash and air-dry your feet and change your socks daily. Also massage your feet to aid in their circulation.
- Clean cooking utensils daily.
- Catholes should be located well away from your camp.

REST
Providing the body with proper rest helps ensure that you have adequate strength to deal with the stress of initial shock and subsequent trials associated with a survival situation.

TRAUMATIC INJURIES AND THEIR TREATMENT

Traumatic injuries are extremely taxing on a survivor, and keeping one's composure may mean the difference between surviving and not. The treatment of traumatic injuries should therefore follow a logical process. Treat the most life-threatening injuries first: breathing, bleeding, and shock.

AIRWAY, BREATHING, CIRCULATION (ABCs)

To successfully treat someone who has a compromise of his or her airway, breathing, or circulation, you must know CPR. Although you cannot learn CPR by simply reading about it in a book, the basic techniques of CPR and clearing an obstructed airway are outlined below. To learn the procedures involved, attend a class provided by either the American Heart Association or the American Red Cross. The techniques that follow are reprinted from *Basic Life Support Heartsavers Guide, 1993,* courtesy of the American Heart Association.

Performance Guidelines for One-Rescuer CPR: Adult

ACTION	HELPFUL HINTS
Early Access	
Assessment: Determine unresponsiveness.	Tap or gently shake shoulder. Shout "Are you OK?"
Activate EMS System	Call 911 or your local emergency number. (Phone first!)
Early CPR	
Airway	
Position the victim.	Turn on back if necessary, supporting head and neck.
Open the airway (head tilt-chin lift).	Lift the chin up gently with one hand while pushing down on the forehead with the other to tilt the head back.

ACTION (Cont.)	HELPFUL HINTS (Cont.)
Breathing	
Assessment: Determine breathlessness.	Look at the chest for movement. Listen for the sounds of breathing. Feel for breath on your cheek.
If the victim is breathing and there is no evidence of trauma, place the victim in the recovery position.	Place the victim on his or her side, using the victim's arm and leg for stabilization.
If the victim is not breathing, give 2 slow breaths (1½ to 2 seconds per breath).	Pinch nostrils closed. Make a tight seal around victim's mouth. Watch for victim's chest to rise. Allow lungs to deflate between breaths.
Circulation	
Assessment: Determine pulselessness.	Place 2 or 3 fingers on the Adam's apple (voice box). Slide fingers into the groove between Adam's apple and muscle. Feel for the carotid pulse.
If the victim has a pulse, perform rescue breathing.	Provide about 12 breaths per minute (1 breath every 5 seconds).
If no pulse, begin first cycle of compressions and ventilations.	Find a position on the lower third of the sternum (breastbone). Compress with weight transmitted downward. Count to establish rhythm: "one and, two and, three and, four and . . ." Depress the sternum 1½ to 2 inches, at a rate of 80 to 100 compressions per minute.
15 compressions and 2 ventilations.	After 15 compressions, deliver 2 slow rescue breaths.
At the end of 4 cycles, check for return of pulse.	If no pulse, resume CPR, starting with chest compressions. If there is a pulse but no breathing, give 1 rescue breath every 5 seconds.

Performance Guidelines for Obstructed Airway: Conscious Adult

ACTION	HELPFUL HINTS
Determine if victim is able to speak or cough.	Rescuer can ask "Are you choking?" Victim may be using the "universal distress signal" of choking: clutching the neck between thumb and index finger.
Abdominal Thrust	
Perform the Heimlich maneuver until the foreign body is expelled or the victim becomes unconscious.	Stand behind victim and wrap your arms around victim's waist. Press fist into abdomen with quick inward and upward thrusts.
Chest Thrust	
For victims who are in advanced pregnancy or who are obese.	Chest thrusts: Stand behind victim and place your arms under victim's armpits to encircle the chest. Press with quick backward thrusts.
Activate EMS.	Call 911.
Check for foreign body.	Sweep deeply into mouth with hooked finger to remove foreign body.
Attempt rescue breathing.	Open airway. Try to give 2 breaths. If needed, reposition the head and try again.
If airway is obstructed, perform Heimlich maneuver.	Kneel astride the victim's thighs. Place the heel of one hand on the victim's abdomen, in the midline slightly above the navel and well below the tip of the xiphoid. Place the second hand on top of the first. Press into the abdomen with quick upward thrusts.
Repeat sequence until successful.	Alternate these maneuvers in rapid sequence: Finger sweep Rescue breathing attempt Abdominal thrusts

BLEEDING (HEMORRHAGE)

Types of Blood
- Arterial: bright red blood, spurting from site (most serious).
- Venous: dark red blood, steady flow from site (serious).
- Capillary: dark red blood, oozing from site (minor).
  Note: Color of blood is not always a good indicator.

Treatment

Direct pressure
Apply pressure directly to the wound for a minimum of four to six minutes. Do not delay in applying pressure even if you have to use your hand or finger. If materials are available, a pressure dressing is very effective. Pack the wound with several sterile dressings and then wrap it with a continuous bandage. Ensure that the bandage is snug, but not so snug as to cut off circulation to the rest of the extremity. (To ensure that this doesn't occur, regularly check the extremity, beyond the wound site, for pulses and sensations. If blood soaks through the dressing, apply subsequent dressings directly over the first. Leave in place for two days; thereafter, change daily. If wound is on an extremity, elevate it above heart level.

Pressure points
Applying pressure to a blood vessel, between the heart and the wound, will decrease the amount of blood loss from the injury site. To be effective, it must be applied for six to ten minutes. Refer to the following diagram for examples of different pressure points.

Tourniquet
A tourniquet is rarely necessary and should be used only when direct pressure, elevation, and pressure points have failed or it's deemed necessary to save a life. Know that the likelihood of losing the extremity is very high. Once you've applied a tourniquet, it should never be loosened. Tourniquets are used on extremities in the following manner:
1. Apply a 3- to 4-inch band between the wound and the heart. For best results, place it several inches above the wound.

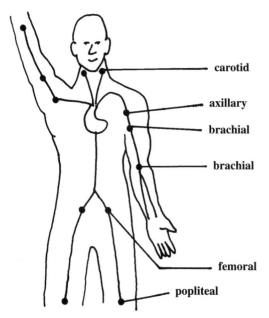

Pressure points can be an effective tool for controlling bleeding.

2. After wrapping the band around the limb several times, tie it into a square knot, placing a sturdy stick in the middle of the knot.
3. Twirl the stick around, tightening the tourniquet until the blood flow comes to a stop.
4. Secure the stick in place and mark the victim's head with a big T. In addition, note the time when the tourniquet was applied.

SHOCK
Shock is a direct result of the body's inability to provide sufficient blood supply to the vital organs. If not corrected, it could ultimately lead to death.

Signs and Symptoms
• Pale, cold, and clammy skin.
• Weak and rapid pulse.

- Restlessness.
- Disorientation.
- Faintness.

Treatment

All injuries, no matter how small, can potentially lead to shock. Victims should be monitored for the above symptoms and treated as necessary.
- Control the patient's heat loss by covering him with any form of dry insulating material and provide insulation from the ground.
- If hypothermia is present, treat it (covered below).
- If the victim is conscious, lay him on his back.
- If unconscious, lay him on his side (in case of vomiting).
- Elevate lower extremities 8 to 12 inches, except when there is a serious head, neck, chest, or abdomen injury.
- For head or chest injury, raise the victim's upper torso about 15 degrees toward a sitting position.

INJURIES TO THE HEAD

Signs and Symptoms
- Bleeding.
- Increasing headache.
- Drowsiness.
- Nausea.
- Vomiting.
- Unequal pupils.
- Unconsciousness.

Treatment of Suspected Head or Neck Injury
- Immobilize the neck if a neck injury is suspected.
- Monitor for any change in the victim's mental status.
- If the victim is conscious, treat for shock by slightly elevating the head and keeping him warm.
- If unconscious, treat for shock by laying him on his side (to avoid aspiration of vomit).

FRACTURES

Closed Fractures

<u>Signs and symptoms</u>
- Site deformity, swelling, pain.
- Inability to move or bear weight on the affected extremity.

<u>Treatment for a closed fracture</u>
1. When in doubt, always treat as if a fracture is present.
2. If the extremity has an open wound present, treat it before splinting.
3. Splint the fracture with available branches or poles. The splint should incorporate the joints that lie above and below the fractured site.
4. Monitor for any changes in circulation or sensation.

Open Fractures

<u>Signs and symptoms</u>
The same as for a closed fracture, except the bone is protruding from the skin.

<u>Treatment for an open fracture</u>
1. *Do not* push the bone end back in.
2. Without handling the bone end, rinse away any dirt and debris with a mixture of sterile water and salt (1 teaspoon salt in 1 quart sterile water).
3. After cleaning the bone and the surrounding area, cover the end of the bone with a clean, wet dressing, using the above solution. It's extremely important to prevent the bone end from drying out.

Suspected fractures should be splinted and immobilized.

During a skiing trip to Steamboat Springs, Colorado, Dr. Robert Wooten demonstrates how to quickly immobilize an upper extremity.

4. Secure the dressing in place and splint the fracture.
5. Monitor the extremity for any changes in circulation or sensation.

INJURIES OF JOINTS AND MUSCLES

Sprains (Area of Pain Is over a Joint)

<u>Signs and symptoms</u>
Are usually the same as those seen with a closed fracture.

<u>Treatment</u>
All sprains should be treated the same as a fracture.

Strains (Area of Pain Is over Muscle, Not Bone)

Signs and symptoms
A strain usually presents as localized muscle tenderness and is usually a result of either overuse or trauma.

Treatment
Wet heat will help increase the circulation within the muscle, which in turn helps in its healing process.

Dislocations (Shoulder)

Signs and symptoms
Shoulder pain with a depression below its anterior tip. In addition, the affected arm is usually rotated slightly outward, with the elbow held away from the side of the body. Attempts to bring the elbow or forearm into the body are met with resistance.

Treatment
If pain medication is available, use it. It's important to find a rock or other formation that allows the victim to lie on his belly with his arm dangling toward the ground at 90 degrees to his body. Tape or tie a 10- to 20-pound weight to the victim's arm (be sure you don't cut off his distal circulation) and let it pull his arm down toward the ground as he lies flat on the rock or other formation. After fifteen to thirty minutes, the muscle should loosen and allow the bone to slip back into its socket. Sling both the upper arm and forearm close to the body so that the arm and shoulder are completely immobilized.

BURNS

Types of Burns (Based on Depth)
• First-degree: superficial without any damage to the underlying skin. Similar in appearance to a sunburn.
• Second-degree: damage into the upper portion of the skin with resultant blister formation. The blisters are usually surrounded by first-degree burn damage.

- Third degree: complete destruction of the skin's full thickness and even deeper. In addition, first- and second-degree burns are usually present.

Treatment

1. Cool the skin as rapidly as possible and for at least forty-five minutes. This is extremely important, since many burns continue to cause damage for up to forty-five minutes even after the heat source has been removed.
2. Remove clothing and jewelry as soon as possible, but *don't* remove any clothing that is stuck in the burn.
3. Never cover the burn with grease or fats, as they will only increase the risk of infection and are of no value in the treatment process.
4. Clean the burn with water (sterile, if available), apply antibiotic ointment, and cover it with a clean, loose dressing. To avoid infection, leave the bandage in place for six to eight days. After that time, change the bandage as necessary.
5. If the victim is conscious, fluids are a must. Major burns cause a significant amount of fluid loss, and ultimately the victim will go into shock unless these fluids are replaced.
6. If pain medications are available, use them. Burns are extremely painful.

FOREIGN BODIES IN THE EYE

Most eye injuries in the wilderness are a result of dust or dirt blown into the eye by wind.

Signs and Symptoms

- Red and irritated eye.
- Light sensitivity.
- Pain in the affected eye.

Treatment

Since most foreign bodies in the eye can be located under the upper eyelid, invert it and try to isolate any dirt, dust, etc. If unable to isolate the cause, rinse the affected eye with clean water for at least ten to fifteen minutes. When rinsing, be sure that the injured eye is lower than the other eye to ensure that the other eye is not contaminated during the rinsing process.

If available, apply ophthalmic antibiotic ointment to the affected eye, and apply an eye patch for twenty-four hours.

WOUNDS, LACERATIONS, AND INFECTIONS
Clean all wounds, lacerations, and infections and apply antibiotic ointment, dressing, and bandage daily.

ENVIRONMENTAL INJURIES AND ILLNESSES
The environment challenges us in many different ways, and it needs to be respected. Realize it cannot be conquered. Adapting and being properly prepared will play a significant role in surviving nature's sometimes awesome power.

COLD INJURIES

Hypothermia
Hypothermia is a result of an abnormally low body temperature.

Ways heat is lost
• Radiation: a process by which heat transfers from your body into the environment. The head, neck, and hands pose the greatest threat for heat loss due to radiation. Additional clothing will slow the process but won't stop it from occurring.
• Conduction: heat is lost from the body when it comes in contact with any cold item. This poses a significant problem when clothing is soaking wet, and in such circumstances the clothes should be removed and changed or have as much moisture wrung out as possible.
• Convection: similar to radiation, convection is a process of heat loss from the body to the surrounding cold air. But unlike radiation, convection would not occur if you were standing completely still and there was absolutely no wind. It's the wind and your movements that cause you to lose heat through convection. Wearing clothes in a loose and layered fashion will help trap the warm air next to your body, which in turn decreases heat loss through convection and also insulates you from the environment.
• Evaporation: heat is lost through the evaporative process that occurs with both respiration and perspiration. Monitoring your activity to ensure

you avoid sweating will help. In addition, if you cover your mouth loosely with cloth or encircle it, the trapped dead air will in turn decrease heat loss through evaporation.

<u>Signs and symptoms of hypothermia</u>
- Uncontrollable shivering.
- Slurred speech.
- Abnormal behavior.
- Fatigue or drowsiness.
- Decreased hand and body coordination.
- Weakened respiration and pulse.

During a cold, wet, and snowy day, Ed Powell fends off hypothermia by building a fire and wrapping up inside a heavy-duty space blanket.

Treatment

Prevention through avoidance of exposure and early recognition are the keys to successful treatment. By dressing appropriately for the environment and maintaining adequate hydration, most problems with hypothermia can be avoided. If hypothermia does occur, it should be treated without delay.

To decrease heat loss, get out of the elements. If wet, change into dry clothes and wear a hat and gloves in order to avoid continued heat loss from radiation and conduction. If possible, climb into a sleeping bag that has been prewarmed by someone else's body heat. The bag will trap the body's radiated heat, and through this process the victim will be warmed. If symptoms are severe, another person should disrobe and get into the bag with the victim. This skin-to-skin contact will provide additional heat through both radiation and conduction. If conscious, the victim should consume warm fluids and carbohydrates.

Frostbite

Frostbite commonly affects the toes, fingers, and face.

Superficial

Signs and symptoms

White or grayish skin that is usually cold, numb, and extremely painful.

Treatment

Rewarm the affected part with your own or someone else's body heat (hands should be placed in the armpits; feet on another person's abdomen). Cover other exposed areas with loose, layered material. Never blow on your hands, since the resultant moisture will cause the skin to freeze or refreeze.

Deep

Signs and symptoms

White-appearing skin that is hard and lacks feeling.

Treatment

The best treatment for frostbite is prevention. Utilizing the COLDER acronym and understanding how heat is lost are two methods of ensuring that frostbite doesn't occur. If your skin should sustain a deep frostbite injury, don't attempt to rewarm it. Rewarming it will be extremely painful, and if the frostbitten area is a limb, it will be rendered useless (you can still walk on a frostbitten limb). Be sure to prevent any further freezing and injury from occurring by wearing proper clothing and avoiding further exposure to the elements. Get to the nearest medical facility as soon as possible.

IMMERSION INJURIES (TRENCH FOOT)
Trench foot is a direct result of long-term exposure of the feet to cold, wet socks. It usually takes several days to weeks of this exposure before the damage occurs.

Signs and Symptoms
The bottoms of feet have the appearance of dishpan hands and are very painful and swollen.

Treatment
If trench foot develops, treat it by keeping the feet dry and elevated. Immersion injuries can be extremely debilitating, so it's best to avoid them altogether. This can be done in the following fashion:

Avoid long-term exposure of your feet to wet and cold socks by changing your socks daily and whenever they become wet. To ensure that your feet are receiving adequate blood circulation, loosen any tight clothing and massage your feet whenever you're resting and/or at night. Pat wet feet dry, don't rub them (rubbing results in furthering the tissue damage).

SNOW BLINDNESS
Snow blindness is a result of exposing your eyes to the sun's ultraviolet rays. It's most often seen in areas where sunlight is reflected off snow or light-colored rocks. The resultant burn to the eyes' surface can be quite debilitating.

Signs and Symptoms
- Bloodshot and tearing eyes.
- Painful and gritty sensation in eyes.
- Light sensitivity and headaches.

Treatment
It's important to prevent snow blindness by wearing 100 percent UV sunglasses. (Refer to chapter 2 on how to improvise sun or snow goggles if no

sunglasses are available.) If snow blindness does occur, treat it in the following fashion:
- Avoid further exposure.
- Place a cool, wet compress over the eyes.
- Take aspirin as needed for pain.
- If symptoms are severe, apply an eye patch for twenty-four to forty-eight hours.

HEAT INJURIES

Sunburn
Sunburn should be prevented by using a strong sunscreen whenever necessary. If a burn should occur, apply cool compresses, avoid further exposure, and cover any areas that have or may become burned.

Muscle Cramps
Muscle cramps are a result of excessive salt loss from the body, exposure to a hot climate, or excessive sweating.

Signs and symptoms
Painful muscle cramps, usually occurring in the calf or abdomen. The victim's body temperature will be normal.

Treatment
Immediately stretch the affected muscle. To prevent recurrence, begin taking salt tablets daily and stay well hydrated.

Heat Exhaustion
Heat exhaustion is a result of physical activity in a hot environment and is usually accompanied by some component of dehydration.

Signs and symptoms
- Victim feels faint or weak.
- Cold, clammy skin.
- Nausea and headache.
- Confusion.

Treatment
• Rest in a cool, shady area.
• Since heat exhaustion is a form of shock, the victim should lie down and elevate the feet 8 to 12 inches.
• Consume plenty of liquids and salt.

Heatstroke

Heatstroke occurs when the body is unable to adequately lose its heat. As a result, body temperature rises to such high levels that damage to the brain and vital organs occurs.

Signs and symptoms
• Flushed, dry skin.
• Headache.
• Weakness and dizziness.
• Rapid, full pulse.
• Confusion.
• Unconsciousness and convulsions.

Treatment

Heatstroke is a true emergency and should be avoided at all costs. Immediate treatment is imperative. Immediately cool the victim by removing his clothing and covering him with wet towels or by submersion in water that is cool but not icy. Fanning is also helpful. Be careful to avoid cooling to the point of hypothermia.

ALTITUDE ILLNESS

Levels of Altitude

As your elevation increases, so does your risk of developing a form of altitude illness. As a general rule, most mountaineers use the following three levels of altitude to determine their potential for medical problems: high altitude: 8,000 to 14,000 feet, very high altitude: 14,000 to 18,000 feet, extreme high altitude: 18,000 feet and above.

Since most travelers seldom venture to heights greater than 14,000 feet, most altitude illness and injuries are seen in the high altitude (8,000- to 14,000-foot) range.

How the Body Compensates as You Increase Altitude
• Increased respiratory rate.
• Increased heart rate.
• Increased red blood cell production.
• Increased capillary production.
• Changes in the body's oxygen delivery capacity.
    Note: The last three reactions are the body's way of increasing the oxygen supply and delivery mechanism. They occur only after several days to weeks of exposure at high altitudes.

Basic Methods of Avoiding Altitude Illness
• Gradual ascent and acclimatization.
• Avoiding heavy exertion for several days after rapidly ascending to high altitudes.
• Low salt intake.
• If you have a history of pulmonary edema or worse, it may be beneficial to discuss the use of acetazolamide (Diamox) with your medical provider. (This is a prescription medication and is contraindicated for individuals with kidney, eye, or liver disease.) The usual dose is 250 milligrams taken two to four times a day. It's started twenty-four to forty-eight hours prior to ascent and continued, while at high altitude, for forty-eight hours or as long as needed.

High Altitude Illnesses
High altitude illnesses are a direct result of a reduction in the body's oxygen supply. This reduction occurs in response to the decreased atmospheric pressure that's associated with higher elevations. The three illnesses of high altitude are acute mountain sickness, high altitude pulmonary edema, and high altitude cerebral edema.

Acute mountain sickness
Acute mountain sickness consists of a group of unpleasant symptoms that usually occur as a result of decreased oxygen sypply to the brain at altitudes greater than 8,000 feet.

Signs and symptoms
• Headache.
• Fatigue.

- Dizziness.
- Shortness of breath.
- Decreased appetite.
- Nausea and vomiting.
- Feeling of uneasiness.
- Cyanosis (bluing around lips and fingers).
- Fluid retention in face and hands.
- In severe cases, there may be evidence of some impaired mental function such as forgetfulness, loss of memory, decreased coordination, hallucinations, psychotic behavior.

Treatment
- Allow time to acclimatize by keeping activity to a minimum for the first two to three days after arriving at elevations greater than 8,000 feet.
- Avoid alcohol and tobacco.
- Eat a light, high-carbohydrate diet.
- Drink plenty of fluids.
- For severe symptoms, if oxygen is available, give 2 liters per minute through a face mask for a minimum of fifteen minutes. If symptoms persist or worsen, descend at least 2,000 to 3,000 feet; this is usually enough to relieve symptoms.

High altitude pulmonary edema (HAPE)
This is an extremely common and dangerous type of altitude illness that results from abnormal accumulation of fluid in the lungs. It most often occurs when a climber rapidly ascends above 8,000 feet and, instead of resting for several days, immediately begins performing strenuous activities.

Signs and symptoms
- Signs of acute mountain sickness.
- Shortness of breath with exertion, which may progress to shortness of breath at rest as time goes by.
- Shortness of breath when lying down. This symptom usually causes the victim to have great difficulty sleeping.
- A dry cough, which in time will progress to a wet, productive, and persistent cough.
- If symptoms progress, the climber may show signs and symptoms of impaired mental function similar to those seen in acute mountain sickness.

- If the climber becomes unconscious, death will occur within several hours unless a quick descent is made and oxygen treatment started.

Treatment

Early diagnosis is the key to successfully treating pulmonary edema.

1. Immediately descend a minimum of 2,000 to 3,000 feet, or until symptoms begin to improve.
2. Once down, rest for two to three days and allow the fluid that has accumulated in the lungs to be reabsorbed by the body.
3. If oxygen is available, administer it, via a tight-fitting face mask, at 4 to 6 liters per minute for fifteen minutes, and then decrease its flow rate to 2 liters per minute. Continue using the oxygen for an additional twelve hours if possible.
4. If the victim has moderate to severe HAPE, he should be evacuated to the nearest hospital as soon as possible.
5. If prone to HAPE, it may be worth trying acetazolamide before the climb. (This is a prescription medication and needs to be discussed with your physician prior to its use.)

High altitude cerebral edema (HACE)

High altitude cerebral edema is swelling or edema of the brain, and it most often occurs at altitudes greater than 12,000 feet. The edema forms as a consequence of the body's decreased blood supply of oxygen, known as hypoxia.

Signs and symptoms

- Signs of acute mountain sickness.
- Headache that is usually severe and unrelenting.
- Abnormal mental function, including confusion, loss of memory, poor judgment, and hallucinations.
- Ataxia (poor coordination).
- Coma and death.

Treatment

Early recognition is of the utmost importance in saving someone who develops HACE. If someone has a severe chronic headache with confusion and/or ataxia, he *must* be treated for high altitude cerebral edema—a true emergency.

1. Descend immediately. If the victim is ataxic or confused, he will need help.
2. If oxygen is available, administer it, via a tight-fitting face mask, at 4 to 6 liters per minute for fifteen minutes, and then decrease its flow rate to 2 liters per minute. Continue using the oxygen for an additional twelve hours if possible.
3. Even if the victim recovers, he shouldn't return to the climb.
4. If he's unconscious or has severe symptoms, all efforts should be made for an air evacuation to the nearest hospital.

SNAKE AND ANIMAL BITES

Snakebites
Very few snakebites are poisonous, and of those, few are ever fatal or debilitating.

Signs and symptoms of a poisonous snakebite
- Fang puncture marks.
- Pain and swelling at the bite site.
- Depending on the type of bite, there may be feelings of weakness, numbness, or paralysis.

Treatment
1. Stop, lie down, and stay still.
2. Remove the toxin as soon as possible, using a mechanical suction device or by squeezing for thirty minutes.
3. If the bite is on an extremity, use a snug band (*not* a tourniquet) that is 2 inches wide and placed 2 inches above and below the site. This will help restrict the spread of the poison.
4. Remove all jewelry and restrictive clothing.
5. Clean the wound and apply a dressing and bandage to the site.
6. Drink small amounts of water.
    Note: Don't cut and suck. This will hasten the spread of the poison and expose the small blood vessels under the aid giver's tongue to the venom.

Animal Bites
Thoroughly clean the site, and treat it as any other open wound.

INTESTINAL PARASITES

Signs and Symptoms
- Abdominal cramping.
- Diarrhea.
- Anal itching.
- Worm and/or eggs in stool.
- Bloody stool.

Prevention
- Never go barefoot.
- Cook your meat thoroughly.
- Never eat raw, unwashed vegetables.
- Treat all water that you intend to consume.

Treatment for Internal Parasites
These treatments are not without risk and should be undertaken with extreme caution. They work on the principle of changing the environment within the gastrointestinal tract, which in turn stuns and/or kills the parasites, which are then passed in the stool. There are two basic methods of treatment; only use one. Mix 4 tablespoons of salt in 1 quart of water and drink. Don't repeat. Or eat one and a half cigarettes. May be repeated only one time in a forty-eight-hour period.

INSECT BITES AND STINGS

Ticks
Remove the tick by grasping it at the base of its body (where its mouth attaches to the skin) and applying gentle backward pressure until it releases its hold. If its head isn't removed, apply antibiotic ointment, bandage, and treat as any other open wound.

Bees or Wasps
If stung, immediately remove the stinger by scraping the skin, at a 90-degree angle, with a knife or fingernail. This will decrease the amount of

venom that is absorbed into the skin. Applying cold compresses and/or a cool paste made of mud or ashes will help relieve the itching. To avoid infection, don't scratch the stinger site.

Note: If carrying a bee sting kit, review the procedures of its use before departing for the wilderness. If someone has an allergic anaphylactic reaction, it will be necessary to act fast. Using the medications in the bee sting kit and following basic first-aid principles will, in most cases, reverse the symptoms associated with this type of reaction.

Mosquitoes
Use insect repellent and/or cover the body's exposed parts with clothing or mud to decrease the number of bites from these pesky insects.

OTHER WILDERNESS PROBLEMS

BLISTERS
Blisters result from the constant rubbing of your skin against a sock or boot. The best treatment is prevention.

Prevention
Monitor your feet for hot spots or areas that become red and inflamed. If you develop a hot spot, apply a wide band of adhesive tape across and well beyond the affected area. If you have tincture of benzoin, use it. It'll make the tape adhere better and also helps toughen the skin.

Treatment
After cutting a blister-size hole in the center of a piece of moleskin, place it so that the hole is directly over the blister. This will take the pressure off the blister and place it on the surrounding moleskin. Try to avoid popping the blister; if it does break open, treat it as an open wound by applying antibiotic ointment and a bandage.

THORNS AND SPLINTERS
Thorns and splinters should be removed, and to prevent infection, antibiotic ointment, dressing, and a bandage should be applied.

DIARRHEA
Diarrhea is a common occurrence in a survival situation.

Possible Causes
- Change in water and food consumption.
- Drinking contaminated water.
- Eating spoiled food or eating off dirty dishes.
- Fatigue or stress.

Treatment
1. Clear liquids for twenty-four hours, and then another twenty-four hours of clear liquids plus bland foods.
2. If no antidiarrhea medications are available, try one of the following:
   - A thick solution of ground chalk, charcoal (or dried bones), and treated water. For best results, take 2 tablespoons of this solution every two hours until the diarrhea slows down or stops.
   - Drink 1 cup of strong tea every two hours until the diarrhea either stops or slows down. The tea has tannic acid, which is beneficial in the treatment of diarrhea. Tannic acid can also be found in the inner bark of many hardwood trees; when the bark is boiled for two or more hours, the subsequent tea is also an effective treatment for diarrhea.

CONSTIPATION
Constipation is another common problem. Don't take laxatives unless it's severe. Exercising and drinking plenty of treated water are by far the best treatment for constipation.

COLD OR FLU
Treating a cold or flu in the wilderness is no different than treating it at home. The problem arises in trying to ensure that adequate fluids, rest, and warmth are obtained. Be sure to protect yourself from the elements.

HEAT RASH
Keep the area clean, dry, and exposed to the air as much as practical.

SURVIVAL STRESS

COMPONENTS OF SURVIVAL STRESS

The effects of stress upon a survival situation cannot be understated. To lessen its severity, you must not only understand it but also prevail over it. The environment, your condition, and the availability of materials all affect the amount of stress you'll experience.

Environmental Influences

There are three environmental influences that directly affect you in a survival situation, and at times, they may appear to be overwhelming obstacles. Many people have perished as a result of unfavorable environmental conditions. In other situations, however, survivors have been successful in either adapting to the given conditions or traveling to another location that was better equipped to meet their needs. Understanding how the environment might affect you is the first step to overcoming the unpredictable hardships of nature.

Climate
Temperature, moisture, and wind.

Terrain
Mountainous, desert, jungle, and arctic (including tundra).

Life forms
Plants and animals.

Your Physical and Mental Condition

Both the physical and psychological stresses of survival will directly affect your outlook and may even dictate the order in which you meet your needs. To prioritize your needs properly, it is important to make decisions based on logic and not emotion. Recognizing the physical and psychological stresses of survival is the first step to ensuring that this is done.

Physical stresses
These stresses are brought about by the physical hardships of survival. Overcoming them requires proper preparation. A good rule for all wilderness travelers is the six Ps of survival: proper prior preparation prevents poor

During training to become a USAF survival instructor, Greg Davenport underwent extreme physical and psychological stress.

performance. Properly preparing involves the following: ensure that your immunizations are up-to-date, stay well hydrated both before and during any outback adventure, and be physically fit prior to traveling into the wilderness.

Psychological stresses
The amount of time a survivor goes without rescue will have a significant impact upon his will or drive to survive. As time passes, the survivor's hopes of being found ultimately begin to diminish. With decreased hope comes increased psychological stress. The basic stresses that affect the survivor psychologically are as follows: pain, hunger and thirst, heat or cold, fatigue, loneliness, and fear.

Availability of Materials
The materials available to meet your needs include both what you have with you and what you can find in the surrounding environment. It's unlikely that a lone survivor will have all the necessary tools and equipment to meet all of his survival needs. The art of utilizing limited resources to meet one's needs is covered later in this section.

OVERCOMING SURVIVAL STRESS
The most important key to surviving is the survivor's will. The will or drive to survive is not something that can be taught. However, your will is directly affected by the amount of stress associated with a survival situation. Prior preparation, keeping a clear head and thinking logically, prioritizing your needs, and improvising all will help alleviate some of this stress.

STOP
When a problem arises, remember the acronym STOP.
1. S: stop. Clear your thoughts and focus on the problem.
2. T: think. Identify practical solutions. Consider each in detail.
3. O: organize. After looking at your options, pick one. Develop a step-by-step plan from beginning to end.
4. P: proceed with your plan. Be flexible and make adjustments as necessary.

Prioritizing Your Needs

Recall the five basic elements of survival: personal protection, signaling, sustenance, travel, and health. Recognizing and prioritizing these essentials will help alleviate many of the fears you may have. The exact order in which they're met will depend upon the effects of the surrounding environment. In addition, your condition, availability of materials, the expected duration of stay, and the given situation all affect how you meet your needs. For example, shelter is of higher priority in an arctic environment than in a mild climate; in the desert, search for water takes on an especially high priority. Take the time to logically plan how to meet your needs, allowing for adjustments as necessary. Through this process, you can greatly diminish the potentially harmful effects of Mother Nature.

Improvising

Improvising is a method of constructing equipment that can be used to meet your needs. With creativity and imagination, you should be able to improvise the basic survival necessities. This will increase your chances of survival and decrease the amount of stress. Following the five steps below will help you logically think out the best method of improvising to meet a need.

Five steps of improvising
1. Determine your need.
2. Inventory your available materials, man-made and natural.
3. Consider the different options of how you might meet your need.
4. Pick one, based on its efficient use of time, energy, and materials.
5. Proceed with the plan, ensuring that the final product is safe and durable.

An example of the improvising thought process
You're lost in a temperate forest during a cool spring evening, it's 8 P.M., and you're in need of a shelter.
1. Determine your need: You need a shelter.
2. Inventory your available materials:
    • Man-made: You have line, a tarp, a poncho, and a large plastic bag.
    • Natural: In the general area, you can see trees, branches, leaves, and cattails.

3. Consider the different options of how you might meet your need:
   - Construct a tarp shelter.
   - Construct a poncho shelter.
   - Construct a shelter using the plastic bag.
   - Find a good tree well (may even incorporate your tarp into the lower boughs to add to the natural protection).
   - Construct a natural shelter using cattail leaves to provide the outer covering.
4. Pick one, based on its efficient use of time, energy, and materials:
   - Time. Options 1 through 4 require little time to construct.
   - Energy. Options 1 through 4 require very little energy.
   - Materials. Options 1, 2, and 3 would require materials that could be put to better use. Options 4 and 5 are good choices, since they spare your man-made resources. Option 4 would use material in an appropriate fashion, provided the tarp was not necessary to meet any of your other needs. Option 4 is your choice.
5. Proceed with the plan, ensuring that the final product is safe and durable: Construct the shelter, ensuring that it meets the criteria in the section on personal protection.

Appendix A

Knots and Lashes

KNOTS

SQUARE KNOT

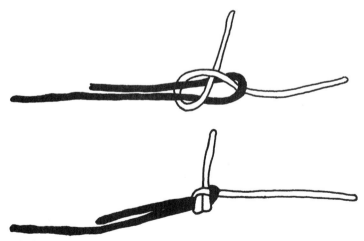

A square knot works best when connecting two ropes of equal diameter together.

DOUBLE SHEET BEND

A double sheet bend connects two ropes of different diameters.

OVERHAND FIXED LOOP

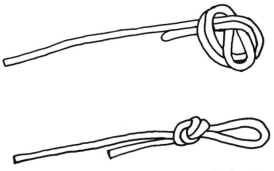

A fixed loop has multiple uses in a survival setting.

BOWLINE

This fixed loop, unlike the overhand fixed loop, is much easier to untie after you use it.

DOUBLE HALF HITCH

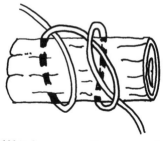

A double half hitch secures a line to a stationary object.

LASHES

SQUARE LASH

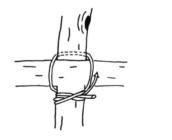

A square lash secures two perpendicular poles together.

SHEAR LASH

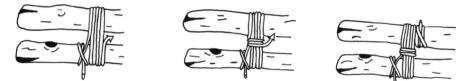

A shear lash attaches several parallel poles together.

Appendix B

Survival and Medical Emergency Gear

Prior knowledge and skill in the basic elements of survival are the keys to ensuring a safe wilderness experience. In addition, proper preparation will prevent poor performance in almost any survival setting and ultimately reduce the amount of stress you might experience. Central to your preparation is an adequate survival kit. This kit will play an instrumental role in how you meet your needs.

SUGGESTED ITEMS FOR A SURVIVAL KIT

Map.   Signal mirror.
Compass.   Whistle.
Flashlight.   Water purification tablets.
Matches and container.   Water bottle.
Extra food.   Plastic bag.
Pocketknife.   Copper wire.
Fire starter.   Fishing line and hooks.
Extra clothing.   Nonlubricated condoms.
First-aid kit.   Parachute or nylon line.

SUGGESTED ITEMS FOR A FIRST-AID KIT

Aspirin.   Matches.
Snakebite kit.   Band-Aids.
Water purification tablets.   Emergency blanket.
Scissors.   Bee sting kit.
Sunscreen.   Antihistamine.
Routine medications.   Tincture of benzoin.

SUGGESTED ITEMS FOR A FIRST-AID KIT (Continued)

Roller gauze.   Various dressings.
Medical tape.   Lip balm.
Triangular bandage.   Soap.
Tweezers.   Antibiotic ointment.
Moleskin.

An SRV-16P survival kit was once carried by USAF fighter pilots. It was small, yet contained several multiple-use survival items.

References and Recommended Reading

Bonney, B. F., and J. K. Drury. *The Backcountry Classroom.* Merrillville, IN: ICS Books, 1992.

Cockrell, D., ed. *The Wilderness Educator.* Merrillville, IN: ICS Books, 1991.

Dawson, R. *Nature Bound.* Boise, ID: Pacific Press Publishing Association, 1991.

Headquarters, Department of the Air Force. *Search and Rescue Survival Training: Air Force Regulation 64-4.* Washington, DC: Department of the Air Force, 1985.

Headquarters, Department of the Army. *Survival: Field Manual No. 21-76.* Washington, DC: Department of the Army, 1986.

Peters, E., ed. *Mountaineering: The Freedom of the Hills.* Seattle: Mountaineers, 1982.

Schad, J., and D. S. Moser, eds. *Wilderness Basics.* Seattle: Mountaineers, 1993.

Schaffer, J. P., and A. Selters. *The Pacific Crest Trail,* vol. 2. Berkeley, CA: Wilderness Press, 1986.

Simer, P., and J. Sullivan. *The National Outdoor Leadership School's Wilderness Guide.* New York: Simon & Schuster, 1983.

Wilderson, J. A., ed. *Medicine for Mountaineering.* Seattle: Mountaineers, 1985.

Index

Page numbers in italics indicates illustrations.

ABCs (airway, breathing, circulation) injuries, emergency treatment for, 140–42

Abdominal thrust, for obstructed airways, 142

Acetazolamide (Diamox), altitude illnesses and, 156

Acute mountain sickness, 156
  signs and symptoms of, 156–57
  treatment for, 157

A-frame shelters, 21, *21*

Agonic lines, *120,* 120–21

Airways, obstructed
  CPR for, 140
  performance guidelines for, 142

Altitude illnesses
  acute mountain sickness, 156–57
  high altitude cerebral edema (HACE), 158–59
  high altitude pulmonary edema (HAPE), 157–58
  how body compensates for increase in altitude, 156
  levels of altitude and, 155
  methods of avoiding, 156

American Heart Association, CPR classes, 140

American Red Cross, CPR classes, 140

Animal bites, treatment for, 159

Animal trails, as water indicator, 63, 64

Animals
  butchering, 107
  gutting, 106–7
  handheld killing devices for, 92–95
  signs of, 92
  skinning, 104–6, *105, 106*
  snares and traps for procuring, 96–104
  tanning hides of, 15–17, *17*

Ants, as food source, 84

Banana trees, as water source, 68

Basic Life Support Heartsavers Guide, 1993 (American Heart Association), 140

Battery and steel wool, as heat source, 43

Beach well, 66, *66*

Bedding, 31
  sleeping bags, proper use of, 12

Bee stings, 160–61

Below-ground solar stills, 71, *72*
  construction technique, 71–72

Berries
  aggregate, *82*
  rule concerning edibility of, 83

Big Dipper constellation, *129,* 130

Birds, 90
  baited hook for catching, 90
  clubbing or catching, 92
  Ojibwa snare for catching, 90–91, *91*
  preparing, 92
  procuring methods for, 90–92
  as water indicator, 64

Bites
  animal, 159
  insect, 160–61
  snake, 159

Bleach, for water purification, 75
Bleeding (hemorrhage)
  direct pressure treatment for, 143
  emergency treatment for, 143–44
  pressure points treatment for, 143, *144*
  tourniquets for, 143–44
  types of, 143
Blisters, 161
  preventing, 161
  treatment for, 161
Boiling food, 107
Bolas, for procuring game, 93, *93*
Bow and drill, 39, *40*
  bow, 39, *40*
  cup, 39, *39*
  fireboard, 39, *40*
  how to use, 40–42, *41, 42*
  spindle, 39, *40*
Bowline knot, *169*
Box traps, 103–4, *104*
Boxing the needle, 124
Braces, fire, 37, *37*
Breathing problems, CPR for, 141
Broiling food, 107–8
Bugs. *See* Insects, edible; Insect bites
  and stings
Burns
  treatment for, 149
  types of, 148–49
Butchering, game, 107

Cacti, barrel, as water source, 67–68
Canadian ace mangle snares, 102, *103*
Cassiopeia constellation, *129,* 130
Cattails, as food source, 77, *77*
Cellular phones, *51*
  as signal device, 50–51
Chest thrust, for obstructed airways, 142
Chop fishing, 89
Circulation problems, CPR for, 141
Cleanliness, health and, 138–39
Climates
  dry (deserts), 6, *7*
  ice, 8–9
  snow, 8
  tropical, 5–6
  warm temperate, 6–8

Clothing, 10
  clean, 10
  double socks, 12
  dry, 11–12
  examining, 12
  gaiters, 12–13
  gloves, 11
  goggles, sun or snow, 15, *16*
  head gear, 11
  improvised, 12–17
  layers of, 10–11
  loose, 10–11
  maintenance, 10–12
  overheating concerning, 10
  repairing, 12
  snowshoes, 13–15, *14*
  tanning hides for, 15–17, *17*
  wet, 11–12
Clubs, weighted, for procuring game, 94,
  94
Cold injuries
  frostbite, 152–53
  hypothermia, 150–52
COLDER acronym, 10–12
Colds, treatment for, 162
Compasses
  circular housing, 120
  establishing field bearing with, 126–
    27
  establishing field bearing with map
    and, 126
  magnetic needle, 120–21
  orienteering, *119*
  orienting map with, 121–26
  rectangular base plate, 119
  see also Maps
Constellations
  north of the equator, *129,* 129–30
  south of the equator, 130, *131*
Constipation, treatment for, 162
Cooking methods
  boiling, 107
  broiling, 107–8
  frying, 107
CPR, basic techniques of, 140–42
Cutting tools, 48
  knives, 48–49
  wire saws, 49, *49*

Davenport, Greg, *139, 164*
Declination, 121
Dehydration, 62, 137
    liquids to avoid, 138
    preventing, 138
    signs and symptoms of, 63, 138
    treatment for, 138
    ways fluids are lost, 137
Deliberate offset, 127, *127*
Desert, traveling in, 136
Desert/shade shelters, *29,* 29–30
Dew, procuring, 65
Diarrhea
    possible causes of, 162
    treatment for, 162
Dislocations, shoulder, treatment for, 148
Double half hitch knot, *170*
Double sheet bend knot, *168*

Earthworms, as food source, 84
Edibility test, 80
    general rules of, 80
    process, 80–83
Edible insects. *See* Insects, edible
Edible plants. *See* Plants, edible
Emergency first-aid. *See* First-aid
Eye injuries
    signs and symptoms of, 149
    treatment for, 149–50

Field bearing
    deliberate offset, 127, *127*
    establishing with compass, 126–27
    establishing with map and compass,
        126
    maintaining a, 128
Filters, water. *See* Water filters
Fire
    banking, 47
    brace, 37, *37*
    building process, 31–46
    building process, summary of, 46–47
    firelays, 44, *45*
    fuel for, three stages of, 32–36, 46, *47*
    heat sources, 37–44
    kindling, 35, *35*
    platforms, 36, 36–37

    purpose of, 31
    pyramid, 44, *45*
    rekindling, 47
    as signaling device, 56, *56*
    site preparation, 31–32
    site selection, 31
    tepee, 44, *45*
    tinder, 32–35, *33, 34*
    tools necessary for building, 48–49
    wall, 32, *32*
Fire ribbon (commercial tinder), 34
First-aid, 140–50
    for airway, breathing, circulation
        (ABCs), 140–42
    for altitude illnesses, 155–59
    for animal bites, 159
    for bleeding, 143–44
    for blisters, 161
    for burns, 148–49
    for cold or flu, 162
    for constipation, 162
    CPR, basic techniques of, 140–42
    for diarrhea, 162
    for dislocations, 148
    for eye injuries, 149–50
    for fractures, 146–47
    for frostbite, 152–53
    for head injuries, 145
    for heat exhaustion, 154–55
    for heat rash, 162
    for heatstroke, 155
    for hypothermia, 150–52
    for insect bites and stings, 160–61
    for intestinal parasites, 160
    for muscle cramps, 154
    for neck injuries, 145
    for shock, 144–45
    for snakebites, 159
    for snow blindness, 153–54
    for sprains, 147
    for strains, 148
    for sunburn, 154
    for thorns and splinters, 161
    for trench foot, 153
    for wounds, lacerations, and infec-
        tions, 150
First-aid kits, suggested items for, 171–72

Fish, 86
    bare-handed catching of, 87–88
    chop fishing for, 89
    nets for catching, 89
    preparing, 89–90
    procurement methods, 87–89
    setting lines for, 87, *87*
    spearing, 88–89
    when to, 86
    when to avoid eating, 90
    where to, 86
Flares, 43
    illumination, 52–53
    lighting and holding technique for, *52*
    smoke, 52–53, 53
Flint and steel, 42–43
    how to use, 43, *43*
Flu, treatment for, 162
Food
    cooking methods, 107–8
    emergency, 111
    need for, 76
    preservation, 108–10
    sources, 76–107
    storage, 110–11
Food sources
    animals, 92–107
    birds, 90–92
    fish, 86–90
    insects, 83–84
    mollusks, *84,* 84–85
    snakes, *85,* 85–86
    vegetation, 76–83
Fowl. *See* Birds
Fractures
    closed, 146
    open, 146–47
    splinting and immobilizing, *146, 147*
Frostbite, 152
    deep, signs, symptoms, and treatment
        for, 152–53
    superficial, signs, symptoms, and
        treatment for, 152
Frying food, 107
Fuel, 36
    kindling, 35, *35*
    kinds of, 36

staging sizes of, *46, 47*
    tinder, 32–35, *33, 34*

Gaiters, improvised, 12–13
Game. *See* Animals
Glass, convex-shaped, as heat source, 44
Goggles, sun or snow, improvised, 15, *16*
Grasses, as food source, *76,* 77, *79*
Grasshoppers, as food source, 84
Ground-to-air pattern signals, 59, *59, 60*
    construction techniques, 61
    patterns and their meanings, 61
    rules of constructing, 59–60
Grubs, as food source, 83
Gutting, game, 106–7

HACE. *See* High altitude cerebral edema
HAPE. *See* High altitude pulmonary
    edema
Head injuries
    signs and symptoms of, 145
    treatment for, 145
Health
    airway, breathing, circulation (ABCs)
        injuries, 140–42
    altitude illnesses, 155–59
    bleeding (hemorrhage), 143–44
    burns, 148–49
    cleanliness and, 138–39
    cold injuries, 150–53
    eye injuries, 149–50
    fractures, 146–47
    head and neck injuries, 145
    heat injuries, 154–55
    hydration and, 137–38
    immersion injuries (trench foot), 153
    insect bites and stings, 160–61
    intestinal parasites, 160
    joints and muscles injuries, 147–48
    life-threatening injuries, emergency
        first-aid for, 140–50
    minor injuries and illnesses, 161–62
    nourishment and, 138
    rest and, 139
    shock, 144–45
    snake and animal bites, 159

Health, *continued*
   snow blindness, 153–54
   survival stress, 163–67
   wounds, lacerations, and infections,
      150
   see also First-aid; specific injuries and
      illnesses
Heat exhaustion, 154
   signs and symptoms of, 154
   treatment for, 155
Heat injuries
   heat exhaustion, 154–55
   heatstroke, 155
   muscle cramps, 154
   sunburn, 154
Heat rash, treatment for, 162
Heat sources, 37
   battery and steel wool, 43
   bow and drill, 39–42, *40, 41, 42*
   burning glass, 44
   flares, 43
   flint and steel, 42–43, *43*
   lighters, 44
   matches, 44
   metal matches, 37–38, *38*
Heatstroke, 155
   signs and symptoms of, 155
   treatment for, 155
Heimlich maneuver, for obstructed air-
      ways, 142
Hemorrhaging
   direct pressure treatment for, 143
   emergency treatment for, 143–44
   pressure points treatment for, 143, *144*
   tourniquets for, 143–44
   types of, 143
Hexamine tablets (commercial tinder),
      34
High altitude cerebral edema (HACE),
      158
   signs and symptoms of, 158
   treatment for, 158–59
High altitude pulmonary edema (HAPE),
      157
   signs and symptoms of, 157–58
   treatment for, 158

Hobo shelters, 23, *23*
Hypothermia, 150
   prevention technique, *151,* 152
   signs and symptoms of, 151
   treatment for, 152
   ways heat is lost, 150–51

Illnesses. *See* First-aid; Health; specific
      illnesses
Improvising, 166
   five steps of, 166
   thought process example, 166–67
Infections, treatment for, 150
Injuries. *See* First-aid; Health; specific
      injuries
Insect bites and stings
   bees or wasps, 160–61
   mosquitoes, 161
   ticks, 160
Insects, as water indicator, 64
Insects, edible, 83
   ants, 84
   characteristics to avoid concerning, 84
   earthworms, 84
   grasshoppers, 84
   grubs, 83
   maggots, 84
   slugs, *83,* 84
International dateline, 117
Intestinal parasites
   preventing, 160
   signs and symptoms of, 160
   treatment for, 160
Iodine tablets, for water purification, *75*
Isogonic lines, *120, 121*

Kindling, 35
   sources of, 35
   wood shavings as, 35, *35*
Knives
   sharpening techniques, 48
   using, 48
Knots
   bowline, *169*
   double half hitch, *170*
   double sheet bend, *168*

overhand fixed loop, *169*
square, *168*
see also Lashes

Lacerations, treatment for, 150
Lakes, location of, 63
Lashes
  shear, *170*
  square, *170*
  see also Knots
Lean-to shelters, *20,* 20–21, *30*
Life-threatening injuries. *See* First-aid;
  Health; specific injuries
Lighters, as heat source, 44

Maggots, as food source, 84
Maps
  colors and their meanings, 114
  contour lines, *114,* 115
  establishing field bearing with com-
    pass and, 126
  latitude lines, 116, *116*
  longitude lines, 117, *117*
  magnetic variation, 115, *115, 122,* 123,
    123
  orienting with a compass, 121–26
  rules for reading latitude and longi-
    tude, 117–18, *118*
  scale, 112–13
  series, 113
  symbols, 114
  see also Compasses
Matches, as heat source, 44
  metal, 37–38, *38*
Meat, drying
  smoking method of, 108–10, *110*
  sun, 108, *109*
Metal matches, 37–38, *38*
  how to use, 38
Milks, Bob, *113*
Mirrors, signal, 53, *54*
  how to use, 53–55, *54*
  improvised, *58,* 58–59
  signaling aircraft with, 55, 59
  signaling on land with, 55, 59
  signaling at sea with, 55, 59

Mollusks, edible, 84, *84*
  mussels, 85
  snails, 85
Mosquito bites, 161
Muscle cramps, 154
  signs and symptoms of, 154
  treatment for, 154
Muscles, strained, treatment for, 148
Mussels, as food source, 85

Natural shelters. *See* Shelters
Navigation
  compass nomenclature, 119–21
  constellations method of, 129–30
  determining direction without com-
    pass, 129–35
  determining general location, 121–26
  establishing a field bearing, 126–27
  map nomenclature, 112–18
  point-to-point, 128, *128*
  shadow method of, 130–33, *131, 132*
  staying on route during travel, 128–29
  tools, 112–21
  using map and compass together,
    121–26
  watch method of, 133–35
  see also Travel
Neck injuries
  signs and symptoms of, 145
  treatment for, 145
Nets, fishing, 89
North
  magnetic, 115, 120, 121
  true, 115, 121

Ojibwa bird snare, 90–91, *91*
Overhand fixed loop knot, *169*

Pace, meaning of a, 128
Phones. *See* Cellular phones
Pine trees, as food source, *78,* 79
Plants, edible, 76
  cattails, 77, *77*
  characteristics of plants to avoid con-
    cerning, 80, *81*
  grasses, *76,* 77, *79*

Plants, edible, *continued*
  pine trees, *78,* 79
  seaweed (sea lettuce), *78,* 79
  universal edibility test concerning,
    80–83
Platform bed shelters, 22, *22*
Platforms
  dead wood, 37
  rock, 36
  snow, *36,* 36–37
  tree bark, 36
Pointer Stars constellation, 130, *131*
Polaris constellation, *129,* 129–30
Ponds, location of, 63
Powell, Ed, *151*
Prime meridian, 117

Rain, procuring, 65
Refrigerators, constructing, 108
Riverbeds, dry, as water source, 66–67,
    67
Rivers
  crossing, 136
  location of, 63
Rocks, for procuring game, 92

Salt requirements, 62
Saws, wire, 49, *49*
Sea ice, procuring, as water source, 65
Seaweed, green (sea lettuce), as food
    source, *78,* 79
Shear lash, *170*
Shelters, 18
  A-frame, 21, *21*
  bedding, 31
  desert/shade, *29,* 29–30
  environmental hazards to avoid con-
    cerning, 18
  hobo, 23, *23*
  lean-to, 20, *20, 30*
  natural, 18–26
  platform bed, 22, *22*
  site selection, 18
  snow A-frame, *25,* 25–26
  snow cave, *24,* 24–25
  tarp, 26–30

tarp A-frame, 28, *28*
tarp A-tent, 26, *26*
tarp lean-to, 26–28, *27*
tent, 30
tree pit, 19, *19*
types of, 18–30
Shock, 144
  signs and symptoms of, 144–45
  treatment for, 145
Signals, 50
  cellular phones, 50–51, *51*
  fire, 56, *56*
  flares, *52,* 52–53, *53*
  ground-to-air pattern, *59,* 59–61, *60*
  improvised, 56–61
  location, 50
  manufactured, 50–56
  mirrors, improvised, *58,* 58–59
  signal mirrors with sighting holes, 53–
    55, *54*
  smoke, 57, *57*
  types of, 50–61
  whistles, *55,* 55–56
Simple loop snares, 99–100, *100*
Six Ps of survival, 163–65
Skinning
  large game, 105–6, *106*
  small game, 104, *105*
Sleeping bags, proper use of, 12
Slingshots, improvised, for procuring
    game, 95, *95*
Slugs, as food source, *83,* 84
Smoke
  black, 57
  as signaling device, 57, *57*
  white, 57
Smokers, *110*
  construction technique, 108–9
Smoking, as food preservation method,
    108–10
Snails, as food source, 85
Snakebites, 159
  signs and symptoms of poisonous, 159
  treatment for poisonous, 159
Snakes, edible, 85–86
  pinning, *85*

Snares and traps, 96
    box, 103–4, *104*
    Canadian ace mangle, 102, *103*
    hiding your scent concerning, 96
    methods, 96
    placement, 96
    simple loop, 99–100, *100*
    squirrel pole, 101, *102*
    triggers, 96–99, *97, 98, 99*
    twitch-up strangle, 99–101, *101*
    types of, 99–104
Snow
    procuring, 65
    traveling in, 136
Snow A-frame shelters, *25,* 25–26
Snow blindness, 153
    signs and symptoms of, 153
    treatment for, 153–54
Snow cave shelters, *24,* 24–25
Snowshoes, 13
    bough, improvised, 15
    trail, improvised, *14,* 14–15
Socks, double, improvised, 12
Solar stills
    below-ground, 71–72, *72*
    transpiration bag, 69–71, *70*
    vegetation bag, 68–69, *69*
Southern Cross constellation, 130, *131*
Spears, 88–89
    forked, 88, *89*
    straight, 88
    throwing, for procuring game, 92–93
    tip, 88
Splinters, removing, 161
Sprains, treatment for, 147
Square knot, *168*
Square lash, *170*
Squirrel poles, 101, *102*
Steel wool and battery, as heat source, 43
Stings, insect. *See* Insect bites and stings
STOP acronym, 165
Strained muscles, treatment for, 148
Streams
    location of, 63, *64*
    as water source, 65
Stress. *See* Survival stress

Sun drying, as food preservation method,
    108, *109*
Sunburn, treatment for, 154
Survival
    availability of materials concerning,
        165
    five basic elements of, 4
    improvising concerning, 166–67
    prioritizing your needs concerning,
        166
    scenario concerning, 1–3
    six Ps of, 163–65
    STOP acronym concerning, 165
Survival kits
    SRV-16P, *172*
    suggested items for, 171
Survival stress
    components of, 163–65
    environmental influences, 163
    overcoming, 165–67
    physical, 163–65
    psychological, 165

Tannic acid, as diarrhea treatment, 162
Tanning hides, 15–17
    process, 16–17, *17*
Tarp A-frame shelters, 28, *28*
Tarp A-tent shelters, 26, *26*
Tarp lean-to shelters, 26–28, *27*
Tarp shelters, 26–30
Tent shelters, 30
Terrain, as water indicator, 63
Thorns, removing, 161
Throwing sticks, for procuring game, 92
Tick bites, treatment for, 160
Tinder, 32
    charred cloth, 34–35
    fire ribbon, 34
    hexamine tablets, 34
    layered forms of, 33
    man made, 34–35
    natural, *33,* 33–34
    petroleum jelly and cotton balls, 34
    wood scrapings for, 34, *34*
Transpiration bags, 69, *70*
    construction technique, 70–71

Traps, animal. *See* Snares and traps
Traumatic injuries. *See* First-aid; Health;
   specific injuries
Travel
   conserving energy during, 135
   contouring during, 136
   desert, 136
   downhill, 135
   four-point checklist for, 128–29
   leaving word before, 136
   packing your gear for, 136
   river crossing during, 136
   scree (small rocks), 135
   situations that suggest, 112
   snow, 136
   staying on route during, 128–29
   talus (large rocks), 135
   uphill, 135
   see also Navigation
Tree cache, 111, *111*
Tree pit shelters, 19, *19*
Trench foot, 153
   signs and symptoms of, 153
   treatment for, 153
Triangulating, 124–26, *125*
Triggers, snare and trap
   figure four, 98–99, *99*
   figure H, 97–98, *98*
   two-pin toggle, 96–97, *97*
Twitch-up strangle snares, 99–101, *101*

Vegetation
   as food source, 76–83
   as water indicator, 64
   as water source, 67–68
   see also Plants, edible
Vegetation bags, *69*
   construction technique, 68–69

Wasp stings, 160–61
Watches, navigating with, 133–35
   north of the equator, *133,* 133–35
   south of the equator, *134,* 135
Water
   boiling, for purification, 75
   conservation, 75
   liquids to avoid as source of, 75
   preparation, 72–75
   requirements, 62
   sources, 63–72
   storage, 75
   see also Dehydration
Water filters, 73
   cloth, 74
   commercial, 75
   seepage basin, 73, *73*
   three-tiered tripod, 73–74, *74*
Water preparation, 72–73
   filtering, 73–74
   purifying, 74–75
Water sources, 63–72
   indicators of, 63–64
   liquids to avoid concerning, 75
   precipitation, 65
   procuring, 63–72
   solar stills, 68–72
   subsurface, 66–67
   surface, 63–65
   vegetation, 67–68
Water vines, as water source, 68
Whistles, *55*
   as signaling device, 55–56
Wilderness traveler, scenario, 1–3
Wood scrapings, for tinder, 34, *34*
Wood shavings, for kindling, 35, *35*
Wooten, Robert, *147*
Wounds, treatment for, 150